Were You Being Served?

Remembering 50 More
Luton Shops of Yesteryear

Bob Norman

The
Book
Castle

First published October 2004
by
The Book Castle
12 Church Street
Dunstable
Bedfordshire LU5 4RU

ISBN 1-903747-56-2

Typeset by GCS, Leighton Buzzard, Beds.
Printed by Antony Rowe Ltd., Chippenham, Wiltshire

Photographs:
Front cover:
S. Barrow, Dumfries Street

Back cover: *(clockwise from top)*
W. Chamberlain
Hawkins Shoe Repairs
Lee's Cooked Meats
Allen's Taxis
G.A. Waller
Cosby's Stores

PREFACE

Bob Norman's previous book about Luton's old shops, "Were You Being Served?", conjured up a warm glow of nostalgia among those of us with fond memories of a vanished town. It became a local best-seller.

The only slight disappointment was that some memorable old shops could not be included. But here, now, is a sequel in which Mr. Norman repairs the omissions. The joy of these volumes is that they remind old Lutonians of so many previous happy experiences. And they are clearly the product of enormous research and local knowledge.

I have a fair idea of the amount of dedicated work such a book involves. The Luton News publishes every week a feature called Yesteryear which includes an old photograph and appropriate details. It's enormously popular but it takes a prodigious amount of time and effort to produce, and woe betide The Luton News if a single detail is incorrect! So I have great admiration for his achievement in discovering so many fascinating and unpublished stories.

Mr Norman has already written about Farmer's, the music centre in Upper George Street. I well remember entering that magical shop to buy the single of Stranger In Paradise, a tune which obsessed me at the time, and being confronted with a list of about ten versions by different singers. The joy of Farmer's was that you could listen to the lot in the sound booths before making your choice. Bing Crosby was mine and I'm still happy with that. Partridge's in Chapel Street (featured in this volume) was like an Aladdin's cave for a small boy. My Mum and Dad bought me a conjuring set with which I briefly mystified my own children in later years. My first student-holiday wages all went on a ferociously expensive cricket bat from G.A.Wild and Son. Lovingly treated with layers of linseed oil, as recommended, it still survives. And a Christmas present for Mum was purchased from Blundell's on Market Hill, but only on one of those men-only nights when understanding assistants would miraculously guess ladies' clothes sizes from embarrassed male descriptions. Those, you understand, were more sheltered times! We journalism students had a routine, after shorthand classes at the old Technical College in Park Square, of dropping into Stalker's in Wellington Street, where there was a stock of Collins' Classics, that handy well-printed series of books with soft leather-look covers. At a rate of one a week, we discovered such treasures as Green Mansions by W.H.Hudson and Under The Red Robe by Stanley Weyman.

But enough of my personal memories. In the following pages is a goldmine of shopping stories and information. I predict another best-seller.

John Buckledee.
Editor,
The Luton News.

For My Family ...

... our link to the past and our bridge to the future

*"The most important thing a father can do for his children
is to love their mother."*

(Theodore Hesburgh)

CONTENTS

INTRODUCTION

The first volume of "Were You Being Served?" was published in early retirement. I did feel that one should not retire not to do things, rather that one should try to do things you may have always wanted to do. Like my father, I love books, not only what's in them, but also visibly possessing them. So the idea of discovering if I could become an author, just locally and however ineffectively, seemed a good idea. After all, it is said that there's a book in everyone! Two years of commitment and then, I must say, it did thrill me to see it in print and I am, of course, indebted to the publishers who, in 2002, took a chance on me. To my constant surprise, it became quite a success. So much so that I was being asked to write a second volume. What? ... find another fifty stories? I really didn't think that was practical. The Luton News review even closed with "Let's hope Bob has enough unused material for a second book on Luton's old shops!" There was no unused material, but fifty more there are in this volume and about forty of them are of differing trades and professions. From the cobbler and the baker to the milkman and the seed merchant. From the newsagent and the ironmonger to the coachbuilder and the taxi driver.

It was, once again, an immense pleasure to meet the older members of the families concerned and in many cases also their descendants. They were all pleased to search their memories and their photograph albums and I thank them for their time and courtesy. Some were old friends, many are now new ones. One hundred stories completed now, with only two refusals to be part of it, but this time even some requests to be included. It has been so enjoyable, nothing equals the pleasure and satisfaction of losing yourself in historical research.

So this second book is once again for those of us who were mostly born before television, credit cards and even ballpoint pens. Do you remember cold bedrooms, when you made toast on a fork by the fire or when crisps only came in one flavour? To us a chip was only a fried potato, young men didn't wear earrings and software wasn't even a word. How the world has changed. So this is recall, reminiscence and recollection. Without doubt if you enjoy this sort of nostalgia, then this is the sort of nostalgia you'll enjoy!

Bob Norman

AUTHOR'S NOTE

"It's only those who do nothing that make no mistakes!" wrote Joseph Conrad. That thought eases my discomfort, as I have occasion to apologize for omitting three valued persons from 'Were You Being Served?', my first local history book published in 2002. The story of Booth's China Shops did not make any mention of the seventeen years of service given by Cliff Richards, who first spent one year in Bute Street and then went on to manage both of their Arndale Centre shops. Frederick 'young Freddy' Harman was missing by name from the Harman's story, although he was perhaps unjustly referred to as the 'faithful porter'. He joined the family firm at the age of fourteen and spent his entire working life there. When Arthur Staddon died in 1938 and the company passed to his widow Daisy, it was incorrect to say that she took little active interest in the business. Mrs Staddon was in the shop daily and continued to run it throughout the war. I ask for their forgiveness.

I would now like, once again, to thank everyone who helped me with their time, and made this second book possible. Special thanks for the support from my family, especially my wife. Without her company and encouragement the task would have been less enjoyable and on occasions it was certainly she who kept me going.

I publicly thank Elvira Adams (EA), Elizabeth Adey, John Allen (JA), Anne Allsopp, Dick Barker, Margaret Barrett (MB), Carol Barton (CB), Bedfordshire County Life Magazine, John Berridge (JB), Peter Bodsworth, Paul Bowes, Pat Boxford (PB), John Buckledee, Jean & Paul Bullimore (JBu), Gwenda & Bill Cavanagh, Bryan Chamberlain (BC), Keith Chamberlain (KC), David Childs (DC), Joan Childs, John Childs, Mavis Clark (MC), Stan Clark (SC), Richard Cobham (RC), Jan Cochrane, Joan Cockfield, Shirley Cooper (SCo), Jack Cornish, Ann Cruttenden, Betty Darbyshire, Madge Dillingham (MD), James Dyer, Carol Errington, Jean & Stuart Farmbrough (JF), Barbara & Martin Felson (MF), Joyce Findlay, David Franks, Eileen Gatward (EG), George Geere, Winnie Geere (WG), Derrick Gilbert (DG), Pat & John Gillespie, Stuart Goodyear, Chris Grabham, Michael Green (MG), Joan Greenacre (JG), Joyce Hafner, Joan & Den Hawkins (DH), Roland Hawkins, Chris Hewitt (CH), Eileen Hibbert, Shirley Hobbs, Janet Horton (JH), Peggy Howe, Chloe Hucklesby, Joyce Hymus, Dorothy Johnson (DJ), John Johnson, Roy Joyner (RJ), Peter Kay (PK), Monica Lacey (ML), John Lee (JL), Clive Lillywhite (CL), Betty Marriott, Ed Martin (EM), Pam Mead, Edna Mills, Tom Mower (TM), Barry Neale (BN), Marian Nichols, Peter Oakley (PO), Terry Olney (TO), John Page (JP), Judy Page (JPa), Ian Pearce, Pauline Pedder (PP), Mike Pierce, Sheila Potter, Elizabeth Pratt, Edna Rippengale, Ben Ripper, Sister Rita Margaret, Theresa Robbins, Jill Robins, Norah & John Robson, Monica Ronald, Clive Rudd (CR), Frank Rudd, Maurice Sanders, Ian Sanderson,

Margaret Sanderson (MS), Vasanti & Chand Shah (VS), Gladys Shortland, Sally Siddons (SS), Joyce Smith (JS), Stuart Smith (SSm), Janet & Geoffrey Squires (JSq), Alison Starsmore of Anglia TV (AS), Vicky Stone (VSt), Phyllis Summerton, Eric Sutton (ES), Ena Tate, Graham Tate, Cynthia Theodorson (CT), Gladys Toyer, Bryan Walduck, the late Phyllis Waller, Tony Waller (TW), Michael Warwick (MW), Roger Wash (RW), Frank White, Jack White (JW), Ken Wingrove, Bob Wood (BW).

Every attempt has been made to correctly acknowledge the photographs, most having come from the families concerned. If anyone feels I have failed to give them credit, I do apologize. Acknowledgement can be seen from initials shown above in brackets which are repeated beneath the photographs. Some were 'Luton News' photographs and some from the Luton Museum archives and I thank them both for permission to use them here. Where no acknowledgement is shown, and errors and omissions excepted, the photographs were either taken by the author or come from his collection.

ABOUT THE AUTHOR

Bob Norman was born in Leagrave, Luton, in 1932. Educated at Norton Road Junior Mixed School followed by Luton Grammar School, he spent two years in the photographic department of 'The Luton News' in Manchester Street, Luton. After National Service he rejoined Home Counties Newspapers at W.H.Cox in Wellington Street. Most of his business life was spent locally in retail photography as salesman, manager and eventually as general manager of University Cameras in Bute Street and the Arndale Centre and later as manager with Lorell Photographics in Oakley Road. He is married with two sons and five grandchildren. In retirement now, this is his second local history book.

The Alexander family that we came to know so well in Luton arrived here from Stevenston on the Irvine Bay in Ayrshire. Peter was the first to come south in about 1860 and his parents William and Elizabeth joined him later, living in Chobham Street.

Peter, who was born in 1828, started business locally as a credit draper calling on customers in Luton and the surrounding villages. As his trade grew he sent for his brothers, one after the other, to come and work for him and later to let them take over their rounds as their own businesses. He also had another interest supplying trimmings to the local hat trade. Peter and his family lived at 140 Church Street in 1881 but traded from 94 Park Street in 1869 and 8 King Street in 1885. He was elected Mayor of Luton for two years in November 1888.

William and Elizabeth had eight children, most of whom came to live in Luton, but it was Peter's brother George from whom the family line descended which produced the Wellington Street shop that came to be so well remembered. George married Luton girl Emily Carrington and they lived in Park Street where their seven children were born. They later moved to "a big old house" in Union Street. Their second child, William George, who was born in 1870, served his apprenticeship with White & Ellis of Ramsgate but at the age of 19 returned to Luton and went into partnership with his father in a new retail drapery business at 33 Wellington Street, trading as Alexander & Son. After a few years he married Lizzie Felks and they lived on the first floor above the shop, where their sons Hedley William and Leonard George were born. Some of the female shop staff also lived in, up the narrow winding stairs on the very top floor where there was also a staff rest room.

Business expanded rapidly and some extension to the premises was made in

1904. No.29A was purchased in 1913 and as Francis Skelton's "home-made boot store" moved to Upper George Street. Number 31 was added, giving them three shop fronts on the bustling Wellington Street. Their large garden, which extended right back onto King Street, contained the workroom where dresses were made and alterations undertaken, with sister Helen in charge. Now with a total of thirty staff, ten were employed in the workroom. Hedley was apprenticed to Joseph Johnsons at Leicester where he met his future wife who was also an apprentice, but he joined the army in 1915, spending most of the time as a despatch rider in France. This meant Leonard leaving school to take his place in the family business. When Hedley returned from the war both sons were taken into partnership, but the "Son" in the company name always remained singular.

The post-war year of 1918 was a good one. Leonard noted in his diary, which he kept for over sixty years, that there was a record rush for the sale and that queues on the first day necessitated locking the doors at 9.30am. "We give you the benefit of a successful bargain", they advertised. "For one week only, 100 jackets in 2 lots at 12/11 (65p) and 17/11

Leonard (left) and Hedley Alexander (PP)

(90p)". They called themselves "The Progressive Drapery House" and "The Noted Glove and Lace House", saying that they were "In the front rank for…gloves, hosiery and laces. On top for…costumes, blouses and ready-to-wear dresses. Sterling value in…blankets, flannels and sheeting". Mourning orders were "carefully and promptly executed, a competent Assistant being despatched to any address on receipt of intimation". Armistice Day produced a big demand for flags and red, white and blue ribbons and 1919 was "a boom year at the shop". No doubt as a result of this, Leonard's diary for May 11th 1922 noted that on this day "our Angus Sanderson car arrived". For only three years in Gateshead this car was assembled from parts, having a Taylor 4-cylinder engine and Goodyear light alloy wheels. An open tourer, it must have looked very impressive, being similar in appearance to the car we all know in Chitty Chitty Bang Bang. Hedley's daughter Betty remembers going out in it and says it was "hood down in the sunshine, then it would rain and all action stations to put the hood up again". In 1919 Hedley had married Dorothy Bollard and six years later Leonard married Slip End girl Hilda Clark, who had been a member of staff until her marriage. Displays were created at all the large public shows held in Luton. The Trade Revival Exhibition took place at the Plait Hall in March 1924 when Alexanders had one stand for fashion wear and one for furnishing fabrics. They also staged two mannequin parades on each of the six days. In October 1925 they gained a prize in the Drapery Section window display competition during the Luton Shopping Festival.

1927 was a busy and important year. William George and his wife moved out of their home above the shop into 'Medwyn' at 98 Montrose Avenue. This released the first floor for business expansion and the Luton Building Company were engaged to make the necessary alterations. The new upstairs showroom at No.31 was for ladies fashions, knitwear and school uniforms, whilst downstairs displayed haberdashery (always known as 'habby'), hosiery and lingerie, which at that time was described

The Wellington Street shop in 1933 (PP)

Seats for many customers inside the shop (PP)

Outings were organised to Wembley and on one occasion two horse-brakes took them all to Ashridge Park for the day.

In 1938 sale items included ladies combinations and cashmere hose both at 2/-, taffeta poults for 2/6, motoring gloves at 3/11 and cloth or tweed frocks for 10/- (50p). The years between the wars produced their best figures but with the coming of WW2 clothing rationing commenced. Throughout this time Leonard was part of the Wellington Street/King Street Fire Watching Rota at his post at Horwood & Boutwoods in King Street. He was also in charge of display for many wartime fund-raising events, The War Weapons Week of 1941, the Warships Week of 1942 and Salute The Soldier Week in 1944. In 1939 Alexanders had produced the first uniform dresses for the Luton Girls Choir, being white taffeta with a blue collar, and every choir member had to visit to be measured for them. The business was converted into a private limited company, Alexander's (Luton) Ltd., in July 1943. Three weeks later William George died, aged 73. Hedley and Dorothy lived firstly in Stockwood Crescent, then Claremont

as mantles and underclothing. While Victoria was on the throne pretty underclothes were not thought of as "nice", but gradually attitudes changed and Alexander's changed with them. They declared that "An Alexander garment is always a thing of Distinction and Beauty". The lower floor of No.33 housed blankets, bedding and materials which formed the Manchester Department. They also made a special study of the fur trade. At this time of enlargement, No.29A Wellington Street was given up and it became the bigger home of photographer William Harold Cox. The Alexanders were considerate to their staff. A family tennis court in Leagrave was available for their use on early-closing Wednesday afternoons. Parties, sometimes for fifty people, were held in the workroom, with staff girls enjoying producing amusing sketches.

Road and finally had 78 Montrose Avenue built at a cost of £700. This was in the 1930s and the house was then on the edge of town next to green fields and they lived there for the remainder of their lives. Hedley was a Rotarian and Hon. Secretary of the Luton & District Chamber of Trade in 1945-48 and President in 1950. Leonard bought 252 Stockingstone Road for £2,000 in 1943, having sold 9 Argyll Avenue for half of that figure. In 1956 he moved to Harpenden but returned to 15 Egdon Drive in Luton in 1973. He served on the Luton War Memorial publicity committee, was a Rotary member and President of The Old Lutonians Club in 1949. Both he and Hedley were Freemasons, Hedley being Master of Stockwood Lodge and Leonard Master of Cumberland Lodge. Leonard was also a founder member of The Old Lutonians Lodge.

Every prospective pupil of the Luton High School for Girls was taken to Alexander's to be fitted with their uniform ready for the start of the Autumn

Ann Cruttenden in her High School uniform supplied by Alexander's (JF)

term, and Jean Bullimore (nee Clemitson) recalls this. She remembers that the requirements in the 1940s were a navy gaberdine raincoat, navy blazer with school badge, navy gymslip, white blouses with school tie, beige lisle stockings, brown lace-up shoes for indoor and outdoor use, navy velour hat with hat-band, long-sleeved beige crossover science overall and a duster, a shoe bag and a satchel. There was no specified clothing for P.E. but it was understood that elasticated pull-on shoes and navy blue knickers would be worn. During the Summer panama hats with hat band and lighter summer dresses were available. Jean recalls

The shopfront at closure in 1966 (PP)

that there were two types of these in differing material but of the same design. One was of a plain gold material with cream buttons and the other in shantung silk with red buttons, but this type became unobtainable in wartime. White ankle socks were worn with the summer dresses. With the exception of the shoes and the duster everything came from Alexander's. The dress varied over the period of the High School existence, but during that time it is believed that very nearly thirty thousand pupils and their parents shopped there for their school uniforms. The Alexander cousins, Betty Marriott who lives in Woodside and Pauline Pedder who still lives in Luton, recall that they naturally had to be correctly dressed. Betty remembers her box pleat tunic and black stockings whilst Pauline recollects the change to the new shape gym tunic in 1939 and her beige stockings. Gymslips had to be checked for length, one inch from the ground when kneeling. They also remember that prefects would check to ensure that all hats were being worn straight on leaving school, and also that they were not allowed to speak to anyone on public transport, not even their relations! The Headmistress declared in the first High School magazine of Spring 1924 that "Old Girls requiring a blazer badge must have a written permission from Miss Sheldon to Messrs. Alexander & Son". Alexander's were also the sole suppliers of uniforms for five other local private schools, Woodlands pupils wore brown and orange, Moorlands had navy and white, those in Westbourne Road dressed in brown and beige, the Convent in Rothesay Road chose navy and yellow and Clevelands pupils wore green and white.

The final twenty years of Alexander's life in Wellington Street saw many changes in fashion, furnishings and staff. Names from behind the counter that may be recalled are Miss Darbyshire, Mr. Dawson, Miss Breed, Cyril Bates and Miss 'Merry' Meredith. It was in 1965, the year that a fashion show was held together with Button Brothers at The Majestic Ballroom in aid of the local charity Ludun, that final arrangements were made to close the company. Hedley and Leonard said "We have no-one to hand the business on to and this is the best way out, rather than sell unsatisfactorily to one of the multiples. We are very disappointed to have to close because the business is probably as flourishing now as it ever was, or even more so." Stock was almost cleared after progressive sales for several weeks and, after a staff farewell dinner on March 29th 1966, one of Luton's oldest established businesses closed on April 2nd after 77 years. The business was sold for £45,000 when the premises were acquired by another Luton firm, stationers and office suppliers Staddons of Bute Street. Hedley died ten years later in 1976 and Leonard in 1984. Numbers 29/29A became, and still are, Sketchley Cleaners. No.31 is currently Alpha Energy Central and No.33 houses Urban & Rural Property Services.

ALLEN'S TAXIS

It was the *fiacres*, the French horse-drawn cabs which were on their roads long before motorised vehicles appeared, that were installed with a taximeter. The meters only became common here with the introduction of motor-cabs and became so associated with them that even now, when we are in need of a lift, we phone or call "Taxi!". For 65 years Lutonians simply called Albert Edward Cecil Allen and later his son John, for Allen's Taxis were synonymous with good timekeeping, reliability, courteous service and of course an exquisite shining limousine with a driver who was very smartly dressed.

In 1902 Albert was born to father Frederick and his wife at 5 Clarendon Road where they lived and worked. Fred as a hat maker and like so many others at this time had his factory in the rear of the house. He kept a pony and trap and often took his family on trips to The Leather Bottle public house at nearby East Hyde. After WW1 the family moved to 12 Alexandra Avenue and Albert went to the Luton Modern School on Park Square. After this he worked long hours in engineering at SKF, often on twelve hour shifts. During the depression Albert found himself out of work and had to find some way to earn a living. In 1925, at the age of 23, with the purchase of a Campion motor-cycle, he went into business carrying passengers in the attached sidecar. He would take you anywhere in Luton for 1/6! Allen's Taxis had come on the scene.

Albert kept a notebook recording his expenditure and income which, together with all the original receipts, makes fascinating reading. The first page tells us that during the first quarter, ending October 5th 1925, some of his costs were 3/- for a week's garaging, 2 gallons of petrol cost 2/10, 1 quart of engine oil was 1/6 and 1 pint of lubricating oil was 6d. His first payment on the motor-cycle was £31/6/0. Finally on this page he writes "Expenditure £64/2/10, Income nil, Loss £64/2/10". The motor-cycle was bought from West End Motors at 233

Albert Allen with his first 'taxi' in 1925 (JA)

Dunstable Road in Luton and I notice that some receipts are signed by R.G.Hickman. It was Reg Hickman who taught Albert Allen to drive and who went on to have his own garage in Church Street, almost opposite the old Fire Station, where the author spent many happy hours in school holidays. The favourite job was laying under the cars spraying the leaf springs with oil, what a mess I got into! Albert also used Lyndhurst Motor & Engineering Co. for servicing. They were agents for Trojan, Swift and Singer cars and said they were "Automobile and Mechanical Experts". From his notebook some interesting purchases arise, such as petrol funnel (1/-), goggles (1/6), Black lead (3d), lamp oil (1/-), clutch wire (2/6), puncture repair (1/6), and charging battery (1/-). The driving licence was 5/-, Hackney licence was 1/-, road tax for motor cycle NM 7471 cost £4 and 2/- was paid for monthly copies of "Hobbs' Luton Time Table" published by T.G.Hobbs, the printer and photographer, from 28 Cheapside. The first week to show an income of £3/0/6 also concludes with a final loss of £13/5/9. It is April of the next year before there is a profit of £4/5/1/ for the quarter. Albert also noted his mileage in the notebook which averaged about 150 miles each week.

In 1929 he married Christine Holt and in 1930 the family moved to 219A Dunstable Road which is when and where their son John was born. Later to No.187A, above Mares clothing shop, and then in 1938 to 21 Avondale Road. Albert had his "stand" by the water hydrant in Beech Road and use of a telephone which was on the outside wall of the Advance Laundry nearby. He is remembered by all for his immaculate appearance of navy suit, black shoes, clean white shirt and black tie, long black overcoat and of course the peaked cap with the highly polished peak. By now he had progressed to taxiing by motor car, and two lock-up garages were used in Westbourne Road. Albert was a skilled but determined driver who would be able, in those years of much less road traffic than we know today, to travel to St. Ives in Cornwall and make the return journey during one night, and often drove to Great Yarmouth and back twice during one Saturday. However his licence does show that in 1938 he was fined 40/- at South Mimms Petty Sessions for exceeding the 30mph speed limit in a built-up area. In the late 1940s the minimum taxi fare was 1/9 for the first mile but private hire fares and Hackney licences were controlled by the local licencing authority, not by the taxi owner. Many years later fares were deemed to include VAT, which brought about applications for fare increases whilst Albert was both Chairman and Secretary of the Luton Taxi Owners Association. The local Police Authority were very strict in their testing of taxi drivers, including placing a matchbox behind the rear wheel which must not be crushed when moving off from a stationary position whilst on hills such as Tennyson Road or Somerset Avenue.

John Allen left Luton Grammar School and joined the staff of the

Albert and John prepare for the Easter Bonnet Parade (JA)

National Provincial Bank in George Street, Luton, until National Service called when he served as a Sergeant in the Pay Corps. However he did not return to the bank in 1950; after all he had grown up with taxis, so he joined his father in furthering the family firm. As expansion took place, John persuaded his father that a larger, more permanent base was needed, so in 1951 they moved into 168 Biscot Road, the resident here agreeing to move into the house the Allens were vacating in Avondale Road. In addition to general taxiing there were emergency journeys to the hospital when babies were on the way, official duties to the Arlesey Asylum when the passenger was often in a straightjacket, and regal excursions to Buckingham Palace garden parties when the limousine and chauffeur cost £12/3/6 return. So very many local weddings used Allen's Taxis at £6/10/0,

including that of the author and his fiancée in 1955, and there were always two highly polished Allen's cars in the Luton Easter Bonnet parades. The vehicles used almost form a history of motoring and John remembers them all, even to repeating, without hesitation, engine and chassis numbers! There was a Delage and there were Daimlers, a Buick GF4558, a Packard AMM314 and a 1939 7-passenger Armstrong-Siddeley BCJ233, three Austin 18s, a 1937 26hp 6-passenger Humber Pullman AMJ268, an Austin Hirecar HTM342 which cost £1000 new, and a 22hp Ford V8 which was bought from Mr. Austin who owned the White Rose restaurants. Then of course there was the graceful 1937 25hp 6-cylinder Rolls Royce DXO417 which came second-hand from Camden Motors. With its James Young body it always looked so magnificent and stately, but

(l to r) 1937 Humber Pullman, 1939 Armstrong-Siddeley, Austin Hirecar and 1937 Rolls-Royce (JA)

then we didn't know that it managed only 12 mpg, that the bumper fell off on the way to Scarborough and that the gear change lever actually came away in the driver's hand in Ivy Road! Pye radio communication was installed in the late 50s with a 100ft mast in Biscot Road. At its height Allen's Taxis had 24 cars in use which included 13 Hackney plates, and a staff of 75 were employed, which included 3 mechanics, 2 in the office and also part-time drivers.

This well-remembered taxi firm of 65 years closed its doors in 1990 and Albert held his licence until this time. He was 88 now and often used one of the large cars for his holidays. He died in 1993 at the age of 91, his wife Christine having died in the same year aged 92. John had been a Freemason, a Rotarian, Captain, Treasurer and President of the South Beds Golf Club and also a member of the Dunstable Downs Golf Club. He is now retired with his wife Klava in the Bedfordshire village of Pulloxhill, enjoying every hole in his almost daily golf.

B. E. BARRETT LTD

Three generations of the Barrett family served Luton well. Arthur Barrett lived at 16 Langley Street for 81 years. He was master of several languages, was also a botanist, an astronomer and a geologist. The Wesleyan Church knew him as a prominent worker, he was a promotor of the local YMCA in Chapel Street and a town councillor in 1886. By profession he was a block maker in the Luton hat trade and produced an ingenious plaiting machine which accomplished work that had hitherto been done by hand. His was a life in which thought for his fellows was an outstanding feature.

His son was Bertram Edgar Barrett who was born in Luton in May 1880, and it was he who was to open Luton's first garage in Langley Street in 1908, it running side by side with his father's wood turning business. Young 'Bertie' had abounding energies and, having determined views and predictions on the future of motor transport, gained a certificate in motor engineering at night school. In 1909 he married Amy Olive Day who had lived in nearby Victoria Street, their son Roy being born in 1913. Olive, as she was always known, had trained as a teacher and a brilliant career as a violinist awaited her, but she opted for Bertie's dream and together they ran his business, Langley Garages, until 1915 when they were able to purchase their new home 'Langley Lodge' in Union Street. Surrounded by a beautiful garden, this was a 200 year old house and was where their daughter Dora was born. With progress they were able to build the vast premises which became Barrett's Garage, partly in Union Street through to Holly Street and also with premises on Castle Street. This came about with financial support from prominent estate agent

The filling station during construction in 1934 (MG)

Benjamin Franklin, who was Bertie's brother-in-law, and also from Bertie's own faith which saw him starting work at 7am and often still in the workshop at 10 o'clock at night. Bertie was an excellent engineer and conjured up many improvements and inventions in his workshop, for in those days it was the practice to repair parts which were damaged. One innovation was the only solid tyre press for miles around. Official repairs were executed for the RAC and the AA. In 1918 they held the Ford agency, prior to The Luton Motor Co. receiving it, and also the sole Humber agency for the area. Their prolific advertisements read "Heated well-lit garage for 200 cars", "Agent for Palladium heavy lorries" and "Biggest Garage in the County". Mr. Dandy's Rolls Royce, Mr. Hubbard's Lagonda and Sir Frederick Mander's big Talbot were all garaged there.

The business became not only a garage for selling and repairing motor cars, which were few and far between in those days, but also a haulage company dealing with parcels and boxes from local hat manufacturers. The hat trade was very busy and there were regular journeys to

The Barrett family pose in the garden at Langley Lodge, 1928 (MG)

collect and deliver boxes of Luton made hats to firms in London. Finished hats were collected from the 300 plus factories in the town which were then sorted and loaded overnight for delivery the next day. Each load was of about 500 boxes. Up to ten Daimler, Palladium, Sedden and AEC lorries formed the haulage fleet which was managed by William Parrott. One day, whilst chatting with Bertie, he wondered how to increase the capacity of the motor trailers which had fixed tarpaulins supported by ash hoops. The idea they had was to bring the body out over the cab and support it with two iron stays fixed beside the radiator, increasing the capacity by 90 cubic feet. The two Luton men conceived the idea for the 'Luton Van', the design being known in this way to this day. It was never

patented. By now three charabancs had been purchased and named 'Busy Bee', 'Buzz Buzz' and 'Bouyant Breezer', with B.E.B. in mind. Evening mystery tours with the chara's proved very popular with the car-less Lutonians.

The business ran for some time in this way, having survived the first world war. In 1929 Bertie's ever helpful accountant, H. J. Cox, recommended that the enterprise became a private limited liability company. The Chairman was Mr. Bertie Barrett and the Company Secretary was his wife. In this year another notable young man, Harold Wilson, worked in, later managed and eventually became a director of the haulage side until it was sold to Stephens Removals in 1979 and he went with it. Sammy Temple who was Service

Interior of the Union Street garage, 1930s (MG)

Manager, joined the Board of Directors at this time, which was also when Bertie's son Roy returned in 1945. Miss Gladys Shortland had joined Barretts in 1919 at the age of 14, intending to stay for only a month at ten shillings a week. She recalls being 'told off' in the first week but replied that she wasn't staying anyway. 'Shortie', as she was known, worked through all departments, eventually becoming Company Secretary, and stayed considerably longer than she planned, leaving after 43 years when she was 57. She still lives locally at the age of 99. Her place as Company Secretary was taken in the 50s by Roy's wife Margaret who had also become a director of the company.

Maurice Sanders, who lives in Eaton Bray, joined Barretts at the age of 14 as an apprentice motor engineer. The necessary 5/- (25p) weekly bus ticket halved his wages, but these rose to £1 in the fourth year. He can recall the 24-hour service offered by the new 'Theo' petrol pump which selected and served eight brands. By the office was a bell button which stated 'Ring for Service'. The moment it rang he had to run, not walk, to assist the motorist. He had a chamois leather solely to clean the rear window and windscreen of up to 100 cars each day. No-one should leave with a dirty windscreen! Impatient clients would drive off with Maurice still performing from the running board, leaping off at the door! This always gave Bertie Barrett great delight. Maurice describes Bertie as a human 'Crypton Tester', who could diagnose most engine faults by listening to the exhaust outlet and who gave him many

hours of tuition in his workshop. Maurice has written about his memories of the local motor trade in his book 'Wood, Wurlitzer & Wesley'. This and his other books have raised thousands of pounds for local charities. I thank him for helping me with this story.

Mention must be made of Mr. Barrett's pride and joy, the 1899 9-seater Daimler which he called 'The Chariot'. He had discovered it rotting away in a field. Making mostly new parts it was lovingly restored and often used as a fund-raiser for local hospitals and the Methodist Church in Chapel Street, even though the method of braking was by pushing a steel spike into the road! The car is now owned by a member of the V.C.C.

Bertie and Olive's son Roy attended Luton Modern School and the City & Guilds Engineering College in London. He worked with a number of companies to gain experience, including the Perkins Diesel Engine Company in Peterborough. Roy and a colleague drove a prototype diesel-engined Hillman car around New Zealand in 1936, hoping to promote business. This was some years before diesel engined cars were on the market. During WW2 Roy worked for the Bristol Aeroplane Company as a flight test observer, sending reports on engine tests back to the factory for adjustments to be made in production. At the end of the war his father was anxious for him to come back to Luton and join the family company. By this time Bertie was 65 and wanted his son to join the Board and allow him some retirement. While Roy had been away, the family, including

Bertie Barrett with his 12hp Armstrong. Inset- Roy Barrett(MG)

Dora, had moved in 1936 to Kinsbourne Green in Hertfordshire. Dora was an artist with a particular interest in horses and at the new home she was able to keep her own pony in a paddock at the end of the garden. Sculpture was to be her life work and her greatest challenge came in a commission to design and create in bronze a work that embodied a Queen and a Cross. Today this work stands in Queen Eleanor's shopping precinct in Dunstable. Dora was also the sculptress of the two bronzes commemorating the Luton Girls' Choir which are on display in Luton Central Library. One is a bust of Arthur E. Davies and the other is entitled 'Singing Girl'. In 1946 Roy married Margaret Spencer from Chiswick in West London, the youngest in a family he had got to know when studying in London. Margaret had served in the WRNS during the war. They also set up home in Kinsbourne Green.

The makes of cars dealt with over the years at Barretts changed considerably. In the early days it was Humbers, Armstrongs and Hillmans. Humber superiority was advertised as having "feather-weight steering of the worm and wheel type which gave confidence at the wheel, even at critical moments in traffic".

Prices ranged between £260 and £860. Next came agencies for Ford, Austin, the 'grace, space and pace' of Jaguar and also the Jowetts. This company made the Bradford van and the Javelin motor car which was very much ahead of its time, but regretfully the Jowett Company did not continue to see as much interest in it as there could have been. By the 1950s, Renault came on the scene and for the rest of Barrett's life that was the car they sold.

In 1969 there was a change in management in that Mr. Raymond Ward, who had been Managing Director of Dickinson & Adams garage in Bridge Street which was by that time owned by Oliver Rix, felt that he would like to join Barrett's. It was agreed that he should come as Manager and a year or so later he was appointed to the Board. He and Roy Barrett were joint Managing Directors and Mr. Bertie Barrett continued as Chairman until his death in July 1971, when his son succeeded him.

So many loyal staff came to Barrett's Garage over the years that it really seemed very much like a large family. So it was with reluctance that the directors decided to call a halt when Roy Barrett was 70, Margaret was 60 and Ray Ward was 65. In 1983, after 75 years, the company premises were sold to Kennings, although they did not want the Renault agency as they brought Volkswagen with them. It is now once again a Jaguar garage in the name of Dunham Jaguar. Roy Barrett died in 1987 but Margaret still enjoys her retirement in Kinsbourne Green.

The genial Barrett family earned the respect of the people of Luton. Bertie was a founder member of Luton Rotary Club and his son Roy was also a member. Both wives were members of Luton Inner Wheel. Mrs. Barrett Snr. continued to play in the Luton Orchestral Society for some years while her husband, son, daughter and daughter-in-law all sang with the Luton Choral Society. B. E. Barrett, 'Bertie', was a remarkable man who made motoring milestones in Luton. He continued to drive until he was 85 and lived to be 91. He was just 5 feet 2 inches tall, but in every other respect this little man was a giant.

**OFFICIAL
DEALERS
for
AUSTIN
and
FORD
CARS & VANS**

S. BARROW

One hundred and forty years ago Phelp's 'The Shopkeepers' Guide' suggested that a grocer should stock fourteen different flavours of tea and sixteen kinds of cocoa. In those days many unpackaged goods, such as cheese, biscuits and bacon, could be bought by the quantity that you personally required and invariably butter was being moulded by patting, right on the counter. Exactly these surroundings existed in Luton in the premises of family grocer Samuel Barrow. He knew what his customers wanted; he specialised in delicacies and I cannot forget the out-of-this-world aroma which came from his coffee grinding machine and which filled the street. The energetic and friendly Mr. Barrow had his shop at 76 Dumfries Street at its junction with Salisbury Road and Buxton Road. (It is now in the hands of grocer R.Johal who has a foodstore, off-licence and launderette there). Known by his customers, young and old, and throughout the trade as Sam, he had a reputation as an expert in tea and coffee blending and he was also adept at boning a ham.

Sam was a Hampshire man who spent two years in Wimbledon before coming to live locally and working in his brother

Sam Barrow poses in his car outside the shop in 1907

John's grocery shop in High Street South, Dunstable. John had previously been a flour dealer in West Street. Sam became well known to the people in the surrounding villages whom he served from his horse and cart for the next ten years. Then in 1896, at about the age of 30, he opened his own shop in Luton. He quickly became the doyen of Luton grocers, being a founder member of the Luton & District Grocers Association and its President three times. There were steps down into his shop which was triangular in shape with long wooden counters on all three sides. Shelves behind them stored large tin vessels for the bulk coffee, flour etc. On the right hand counter dairy products, butter and eggs were on sale and there was a large hand-operated bacon slicer and it was the customer who decided how thick he wanted the rashers. Sugar was packed in thick dark blue bags. Along the front of this counter was a row of square biscuit tins, all angled towards you so that you could see the different types easily, and the tin containing the broken biscuits was always a favourite. Sam was always in his long spotless white overall. He could always go to a top shelf and fulfil the most unusual request, such as Kruschen Salts

ALL COFFEES ARE ROASTED DAILY ON THE PREMISES –

REMEMBER IT MUST BE BARROW'S

Rich aroma distinctive Flavour and strength

BARROW'S STORES, BUXTON RD., LUTON

(good health for a farthing a day), Seccotine (in pin-stopper tubes), Dr.Cassell's Tablets (for ill-nourished nerves) or tins of Oakey's Knife Polish.

His shop and cellar were, like Sam, a wonderful example of method and cleanliness. All his staff gave long service, at one time they had given him an aggregate employment of 176 years. All his life, indeed into his late 80s, Sam appeared for work promptly at 8.30 every morning and rarely left before 6.15, and then often carrying boxes of groceries to deliver to customers who lived nearby. Then he would attend to business matters during the evening at his home at 46 Napier Road. This was a three storey house with a small scullery and kitchen to the rear which is now called Napier Court. He employed a housekeeper to do the housework and prepare his meals. A friend of mine who lived next door recalls that their rent was 14/- a week. She remembers that when not at the shop, gardening seemed to be Sam's life and he could often be seen attending to his wonderful display of dahlias which filled the three tiers of his front garden and the long rear garden which backed right up to the cemetery wall. My wife, who lived nearby, would respond to a request from

Miss Toyer who was housebound in Napier Road and who lowered her shopping basket on a rope from the first floor of her house. When the groceries had been purchased from Barrow's, the basket would be hoisted up again in the same way.

Sam, a bachelor, was well-known as a lecturer on many subjects including astronomy and poetry. He could entertain from the works of Shelley, Keats, Wordsworth and Byron. His memorable bygone shop traded here for sixty years and now gentleman Sam has gone. I wonder if he quoted this Byron, "I die – but first I have possessed. And come what may, I have been blessed" …That was Sam.

Sam Barrow

BERRIDGE'S COMMERCIAL SCHOOL

Phonography is the art of representing each spoken sound by a distinct character. It's what we would call shorthand. Sir Isaac Pitman was the inventor of the shorthand known by his name and he gave his lifetime to spreading the use of his system worldwide. Phonography and shorthand are words little used nowadays but, together with a typewriter used in accepted office practice, they formed a cornerstone in the life of wordperfect Gladys Agnes Berridge.

Gladys Stafford was born in Leicester in 1904 and the family home was in

Gladys Berridge (JB)

Stoughton Street. She attended the local elementary school, leaving at 14 and returning for evening classes to learn the new-fangled arts of shorthand and typing. They were a poor family, Gladys's mother taking in sewing at home. She sewed the buttons on army trousers at a farthing a time, a farthing for each pair of trousers, that is! Gladys's hard work eventually won her letters after her name, P.C.T., or Pitman's Commercial Teacher, almost unheard of now. It was what would be called today the industry standard, for a Pitman's certificate became the required qualification for anyone wanting to be a shorthand typist or secretary and the strongly preferred qualification for a journalist. Gladys married Steven Arthur Berridge who came from Bulwell in Nottingham. He came from a family who were all employed in a very successful little family empire built on the recycling of waste products. There were six sons who each ran one part of the business. Steven ran the waste materials from the clothing trade which supported two shops selling clothes too good to be recycled. Unfortunately the brothers fell out and Steven and Gladys moved south to make a fresh start.

They lived in Stevenage, then a sleepy market town, where Steven was what was then usually called a 'garage man'. He did repairs and bought and sold cars, which was at that time a somewhat difficult way of making a living. Moreover he was not a very good business man; he was a car cognoscente, quite likely to say to a customer who was enquiring about a second-hand Austin, "Never mind that,

The class of 1947 (EA)

we'll do that in a minute, just come and listen to the engine of this Rolls Royce that's just come in." Gladys, like most married women in those days, was not working but she had a background which was to prove a major influence on the lives of the family. In 1927 their son John was born, and a year later the family moved to Luton, mainly to afford more scope in Steven's business. They moved into 1 Mansfield Road, chosen because a wide drive led from the front to a huge hanger-like garage at the back. In a few years another move was made to 355 Dunstable Road which had a garage nearby which Steven called Car Mart and later to Church Street, opposite the old Fire Station. By the time she moved to Luton, Gladys had of course achieved the

P.C.T. standard, high levels of competence in shorthand, typing and book-keeping and some years experience in business. Little did she know how important this was to be within a decade. In the mid 1930s Gladys drifted into teaching her skills, to friends at first, but she turned out to be an excellent teacher and soon complete strangers were coming to ask if they could join "the classes". The demand soon became large enough to require a move to a larger house and in 1934 they rented 44 Dunstable Road on the corner with Collingdon Street, for buying was rare in those days. It was a large Victorian house entered from the front in Dunstable Road up a short flight of steps. At that time it was opposite Dunstable Road School and Henry

Brown's timber yard. Next door at 44A was the substantial house of Mr Charles Bird, the owner of Charles Bird & Sons, the builder's merchants in Collingdon Street. Next at 42 was Dr Lloyd's and a little further up at number 34 was "The Fox" public house. All these are gone now, demolished to assist in building the new road layout at the junction of Dunstable Road and Hatters Way. I guess that 44 Dunstable Road would have been where the large roundabout is now at the junction of Dunstable Road and Hatters Way. For the next two years there were two incomes coming in, family life was a little easier and the business grew rapidly. Berridge's Commercial School made its existence manifest by a large sign erected in the tiny front garden so that it faced Collingdon Street and Dunstable Road, and therefore was particularly visible to all the town-bound traffic. Number 44 had a large front room and an equally large back room, divided by double doors which could open to provide a much larger room when necessary, and these two rooms provided the necessary teaching space. The downstairs living space was one smaller room and the kitchen. The front room became known as "The Typing Room" and the back room "The Shorthand Room", where the third commercial skill, book-keeping, was also taught. Day and evening the front garden was full of the girls' bicycles, nobody had a car of course, so all the pupils came on foot, by bike, by bus or by train, for some of them came from as far away as Bedford. The bikes were never padlocked and no-one can recall one being stolen.

Two years later, in 1936, Steven was diagnosed with cancer of the spine. In those days very little was known of the problem, little could be done to help, so he was in great pain and soon confined to bed. Hard times were ahead as Gladys tried to combine the business of the school with nursing her husband. The school, which was now growing to the point at which one of the bedrooms had to be pressed into service as a third classroom, with some of the best students being employed as teachers once they qualified, now had to support the family and also Gladys's mother who lived with them and whose main concern was looking after her grandson John. Steven's illness was of course very expensive, there being no National Health Service, and visits to, or house calls from, the doctor meant a fee, and because of the serious nature of the illness even more expensive consultants' and hospital fees were involved. Steven Berridge, who was 21 years older than Gladys, died in 1938, aged 55. It is of immense tribute to Gladys Berridge that she brought her family through that period of two years of intense physical and financial strain and continued to build her school into a business widely respected in Luton and throughout a much wider area. She would be up early in the morning to clean and prepare the schoolrooms; no central heating in those days, so fires had to be laid in every room and coal carried up from the cellar. She then taught classes through the day until late in the evening. For a while she supplemented her income by running postal tuition courses, often sitting up in bed marking the work of her correspondence course pupils. Nor was she merely a teacher. In a wartime society devoid of social services, employment agencies, moral welfare services and leisure activities, she played a role in these spheres as well. When her 'girls' graduated she helped find them jobs and made sure they were properly remunerated and treated. Businessmen telephoning for a typist or book-keeper soon found she was not be trifled with. "Oh no, she's worth more than that, I think you must give her at least ten shillings a week!" She was fiercely defensive of her younger students' welfare. It is known that once during the war she learned that one of her younger girls was going out with an American serviceman. The girl's mother having sought her help, Gladys went into the town, called the American and the girl out of the bus queue outside the Carnegie Library and read him the riot act. "Do you know how old this girl is?" To be fair he probably didn't, but it made other girls think twice before getting into similar relationships. She helped the girls find things to do in the fairly austere wartime existence. A keen tennis player herself, she rented some courts and a large shed with tea-making facilities and provided a tennis club for her girls. On Wednesday afternoons she would take the girls out for a bike ride and a picnic. Throughout the war years the school never closed, though on several occasions the early classes were delayed when the windows had been blown in by nearby bombs during the night and all the glass had first to be

swept up. Mrs.Berridge was punctilious about keeping the school up to date. As soon as the first duplicator was on the market, she had one, a simple box with a silk screen over which you ran a thing like a paint roller primed with a particularly unpleasant black sticky ink and the use of this was incorporated into the classes. The first rotary duplicator came as well and the dictating machines, together with a collection of gadgets like shorthand machines which were supposed to revolutionise the commercial world but never really caught on.

Chloe Hucklesby (nee Lawrence) lived in Stuart Street and her parents and the Berridge family were good friends, often playing tennis together in Wardown Park. Chloe went to the Commercial School in 1946, passed all the exams, continued secretarial training at the Luton Chamber of Commerce in George Street West and gained a permanent position there. She is now living in New Zealand and says "Mrs Berridge was an excellent tutor for shorthand typing and book-keeping." Pam Mead (nee Mills), who lives in Stotfold with her husband Des, joined Mrs Berridge as a part-time student, attending evening classes in 1946 and 47. Her sister Edna had been there before her, so it seemed the right thing to do as she wanted to work in an office, and shorthand and typing was not taught in Secondary Schools at that time. She recalls that on entering the classroom one could not call it luxurious. "In the typing room were rows of small desks, each holding a typewriter which nowadays would be in a museum. The old heavy

Imperial and Corona were there for us to learn on, all with a black cover to keep out the dust and which had to be replaced at the end of class. We had to buy a book to help us learn the keyboard and, once this was done, we had a cover over the keys, hands underneath, and away we went reading from side to side and typing without looking at the keyboard. Next came the shorthand lesson which I likened to learning another language. The signs for all words were above, on or below the line and with thick or thin lines, curves, dots, dashes etc. Speed in writing the signs was the object to be achieved. Book-keeping was also studied and all this took about two years. Mrs Berridge was a good teacher and now we can appreciate the help she gave us in obtaining a start in our chosen career."

Elvira Adams (nee Jones), who can be seen second from right in the back row of our class photograph, has good memories of her two years spent at this prestigious secretarial school, so many good memories that she was able to recall them all for publication in "Bedfordshire County Life" magazine in 2000. Elvira took the two year course in shorthand, typing, business management and accountancy in 1947. She says "Learning to type was the easy part, while shorthand skills were quite hard to master. I practiced my shorthand speeds by writing the words of songs I would listen to on the wireless, this being a favourite pastime. I recall my satchel weighing me down with accountancy journals, sales ledgers, cash inwards and outwards books, statements of accounts, etc." Mrs.

Berridge's brother lived next door to Elvira in Mayne Avenue, Leagrave, but this association did not give her an easy time. She recalls Mrs. Berridge telling her that her own 85 year old mother could spell and write better than she could! Elvira remembers one hot summer's afternoon in 1948 when she was taking a typing exam. She says "The windows in the room were wide open and the smell of chocolate wafted into the classroom from the local cocoa factory in Dallow Road which, if the wind was in the right direction, would fill Berridge's and our nostrils with this wonderful smell. I'm sure it was that afternoon back in 1948 which is responsible for the chocoholic I am today!" Towards the end of the course Elvira complemented her training in the administration office of the Luton Technical College, with Shaw & Kilburn and the Luton Chamber of Commerce before becoming a secretary for eight years with Blundell Rules Ltd. in Chaul End Lane. "Tippex," she says, "was unheard of then and any mistakes would be rubbed out with a special rubber which would always make a terrible mess because you would need to blow away the little bits of rubber before they fell into the typewriter and clogged up the keys." Elvira, who now lives in Swansea with her husband Brian, says she is proud to have been at Berridge's and writes "I can confidently say that all students held Mrs. Berridge and her school in high regard. She would have been very proud of us all and in turn we would never have let Mrs. Berridge or our school's good name down."

The School at the corner of Dunstable Road and Collingdon St

The School provided a service and filled a need at a time when there was virtually no 'commercial' education provided, and it is estimated that about sixty girls passed through the school each day. Eventually, however, the Technical College in Park Square got around to the idea of introducing the same sort of classes as Berridge's was providing – free of charge! Gladys knew from the start that she would not be able to compete with this once the classes were established and had gained a reputation. Fortunately the College realised that if it had her on board rather than as a competitor, the process of establishing the commercial classes would be much easier. They offered her an assistant lecturership, which she accepted. This gave her a salary, the ability to continue teaching

and now some time of her own. She had a house built at 45 Hilary Crescent and was able to enjoy quite a large garden. A bus stopped nearby to take her to College each day until she was over seventy. In retirement she was able to spend time with her son John, his wife Margaret and family in Dundee but lived in Luton until she was eighty-six, when she agreed to move to Scotland and into a well-appointed Retirement Home. The ordered routine of an old people's home sat very uncomfortably with someone who had been captain of her own affairs for most of her life. She died there, peacefully, in 2002, in her ninety-eighth year. Her son John worked at Luton Hoo, the Davis Gas-Stove Co and AC-Sphinx at Dunstable before going to King Alfred's College at Winchester and the London School of Economics. He was consultant to the Edward Heath shadow cabinet working party on devolution for Scotland and eventually held the post of Senior Lecturer in Politics and Jean Monnet Lecturer on the European Community at the University of Dundee before retirement.

C Madge Cardall

In the Black Forest, in 1872, Karl Nessler introduced the first permanent wave for ladies' hair and in the same year Marcel Grateau conceived his Marcel Wave. The perm had arrived and, although it meant a lengthy visit to the hairdresser, it became the height of fashion for many decades. In Luton, in the 1930s, the Cardall sisters, Vera and Madge, saw as many changes in their shops as the hairstyles that were emerging from them.

Coventry born Sam Cardall played violin in all parts of the country and was well-known locally in the orchestras that regularly played at the Alma, Palace and Grand Theatres in Luton. Sam and his wife, Minnie, lived in John Street where their daughters were born and where Minnie, as a favour, accommodated performers from the theatres. Madge attended Christ Church School and Beech Hill School when the family moved to Durbar Road. Leaving school at 14 she first took a millinery

Madge Cardall (MD)

apprenticeship with Currant & Creak in Bute Street. Vera was the first to open her ladies' hairdressing salon at 29 Collingdon Street in 1933, Madge joining her shortly after, and they worked together for nearly three years. However, when Madge was 19, she longed to open her own salon and asked her elder sister if this would be acceptable. Vera replied with a grin, "everyone can be done without!" So in 1935 Madge commenced her own business further along Dunstable Road, in Inkerman Street. Her Auntie, Florence Allen, bought the building and let it to Madge. Originally a three-storey house with a basement, it was converted into a shop by builder Bert Wilkes who was her sister Vera's husband. Business continued during these alterations, but unfortunately the lady customers had then to be helped up a fairly high ladder to the second floor, some older ones needing assistance from the workmen, it all creating many laughs.

At this time, before hood driers were installed, hair was dried using hand driers, and Marcel Waving was the most popular request, which was hard work for the staff. Later there were heated perms and then the chemical cold perms. A Marcel Wave in 1935 cost 1/- (5p), a shampoo and set was 2/6d and a tanner extra was charged for the 'special shampoo'. Cold perms were to cost 21/-. They could take up to half a day, but the ladies always thought it was worth it. A perm was needed at later intervals which would usually be six to nine months. Originally the salon layout in Inkerman Street was with a separate cubicle for each washbasin, sometimes referred to as 'confessionals', but the need for gossip

57 Inkerman Street (MD)

prevailed and they were later removed. Only one cubicle remained, for use when hair was being dyed. Among staff who may be remembered are Betty Pedley, Ann Barker, Janet Overthrow and Hilda Tyler. Many of the business ladies of the town were customers, Mrs Blows, Mrs Sapsford and Mrs Farmer being particularly remembered.

During WW2 Madge made large bonnets for her customers to wear, just in case an air-raid took place during their perms and they had to run to the shelter which was just up the road. In 1941 Madge married Keith Dillingham who came from an eminent local hat manufacturing family. Her maiden name remained on the salon in which a surprising departure took place in 1960.

Madge opened a poodle parlour on an upper floor which was successful for the next ten years. Sometimes they were attending to the dog upstairs and its owner downstairs!

After 35 years in business, Madge retired in 1970 and she still keeps in touch with some of her past employees. Retirement brought enjoyment of world travel with Keith. They still live in Luton and have now celebrated their diamond wedding anniversary. Number 57 in Inkerman Street remains in the business of hair fashion, it now being Tony & John's Unisex Hairdressing. Speaking of today's ladies' hairstyles, Madge, now in her 88th year, says that she still prefers the old styles but accepts that fashion has to move on.

Staff (l to r) Hilda Tyler, Madge Cardall, Brenda Chorley and Florence Allen (MD)

'Mr. Teasey Weasey' demonstrates to Luton hairdressers in the Luton Town Hall, 1950s (MD)

W.
Chamberlain

Walter Chamberlain of 36 Buxton Road in Luton was 23 years old when, in 1895 with Rev. O'Neil at St. Mary's Church, he married Annie Adams who was four years older than Walter. They both came from upright families, Walter's father being an insurance agent and Annie's father a local tailor. They set up home at 103 Park Street, but the heartbreak is that Walter was to have only another seventeen years to live. However they were blessed with six children, May, Ivy, Alfred, Horace, Ernest and William. Walter was Church Warden at Luton Parish Church and on Sundays could be seen walking his children along to St. Mary's, always wearing his silk top hat. He was self-employed as a plumber and decorator at Park Street where he also had his first general hardware shop. Deliveries were made by handcart and horse and cart, these being stabled through the large gateway adjacent to the shop. Even then the stock was quite varied, for they advertised on the door "Cheapest House for Mantles, Globes, Burners etc." and a WC pan is included in the window display. In 1909, at the age of 37, he opened his second shop at 106 Dunstable Road, which had previously been Miss Ashton's fancy

Walter and William Chamberlain (KC)

drapery shop. General hardware sales were again his line and with this success, in 1911, the family moved nearer to the shop with a house at 71 Hazelbury Crescent. Advertising boards were displayed on the upper floor declaring their abilities. They were sanitary plumbers supplying hot and cold water fittings, painters, glaziers and house decorators, varnish merchants, and the boards promoted lead glass, electric bells, gas fittings and 'brushes and brooms of every description'. Along the same parade of shops they also ran a tailors and outfitters which had previously been Mr. Neville's. Mr.B.Cornish was the Manager who always had a good display of straw boaters in the window and was proud to sell British Braces.

Walter was successful in advancing his enterprise but tragedy struck in 1912 when he died at the age of 40. The family had to very quickly re-organise their lives and a Company was formed with May, Ivy, Ernest and William as partners in order to continue support for their mother. Alfred had died in his twenties following a motor-cycle accident and Horace, who sadly was a little handicapped, was unable to take the responsibility, but did become very useful in the shop. Harold Deadman was taken onto the staff as shop manager and filled this position creditably for about thirty years. He was a short, portly gentleman who spent his working days in his apron and invariably wearing his bowler hat. When his retirement came, it was Walter's son William, an electrician by trade, who changed direction in 1950 and filled his father's shoes in the family business. William had married Phyllis Shaw, and their son Bryan still lives in Luton. Their daughter Pauline lives in Norfolk. Ernest had married Winnie Lawrence and their son Keith also still lives in Luton. Both William and Ernest and their families lived in St. Mildred's

103 Park Street, Luton (KC)

Avenue. Bryan, who had previously worked with Gibbs & Dandy, joined his father for two separate periods but they were often unrewarding times. Keith also helped out on Saturdays delivering customers' paraffin on the company bicycle. Jack Chote worked with Chamberlain's for many years and also Cliff Garrett until he left to become a full-time Captain with The Salvation Army.

The vast range of stock that an ironmonger or hardware dealer has to keep rules the layout of the shop and every inch of space is filled with his wares. Chamberlain's was long and narrow, with an uncovered wooden floor and a wooden counter of only about four feet width, even this holding display shelves on the right and the cash till on the left. Of course screws and nails were stocked and they could be purchased in the exact quantity required. Stock was bought from Oakleys and Sterns, the London wholesalers, who specialised in pots and pans and crockery. There were large stocks of casement stays and antique door knockers which were known as 'black ironmongery', and locks of all types were also always

available. Local plumbers and George Kent's were valued customers and schools were supplied with their necessary cleaning materials. The lack of display space was solved by letting the goods extend out onto the pavement, so every day wheelbarrows, fireguards, dustbins, buckets, brooms and bungalow baths were assembled outside the shop. A trolley containing peasticks and bamboo canes

106 Dunstable Road, Luton (KC)

was also wheeled outside and in later years a display of 'Addis' products was included. It took a good half-hour to do this at the start and end of each day and this was usually Horace's job. Next door to this busy shop was Henry Inwood's, the provision merchants and next to this was Davis's Linen House. After WW2 Inwood's became W.H.Cullens and the Waldeck Café was then on the corner.

In 1973, when the building was coming into disrepair and buckets from stock were being used to catch the internal rainwater, William retired. This brought to an end, after 64 years, one of Luton's highly regarded hardware dealers. Chamberlain's were in the busy Dunstable Road shopping area, very near to the ground of Luton Town Football Club. If Chamberlain's were unable to supply the item you wanted, they would always get it for you, suggesting 'Call again at the next home match!'

Chamberlain's tailor's shop in Dunstable Road (KC)

W. CHILDS LTD

There cannot be many Lutonians who can remember a long line of horse-drawn wagons standing in Collingdon Street. They would be seen near number 62, which is where Mr. Hawkes was the local wheelwright. Our story here tells of a Bedfordshire man who was himself a trained wheelwright and who joined Mr. Hawkes after his WW1 service on the Somme in France. However whilst he worked on the wagon wheels, he had a firm belief in the future of the motor car and went on to become a motor body builder, repairer and coachpainter second to none in Luton.

William Childs was born in High Street, Toddington in 1896. His father, also William, was a ploughman and agricultural worker. William jnr. left the National School, Toddington, at 14 when he was apprenticed to the village undertaker and wheelwright, Mr Timms.

On leaving the army, William 'put his shoulder to the wheel' and came to work at Hawkes in Luton every day. William moved from an employee to partner in 1920 and continued to work not only on wagons and trolleys but also on the bodies of a few motor vehicles. Travelling to Luton meant riding his trusty Swift motorcycle and it is recalled that sometimes, particularly with a pillion passenger, he had a problem going sufficiently fast to lose the dogs which liked to chase it! In 1920 William was married to local girl Emily Ansell in Toddington and they moved into a cottage on the High Street where William, Derrick, and Mary were born. Realising that the days of the wheelwright were numbered, he decided to branch out on his own and rented premises in Frederick Street Passage where he started a coachbuilding and coachpainting business where he would build, repair and paint motor vehicles. W.Childs' day book of the time still exists and makes engaging reading. Over two years 350 jobs are

(l to r) William, Derrick, John and David Childs (DC)

recorded, for example to West End Motors 'Writing numbers on Singer Saloon 3/6'. Also for them, 'Straightening and beating out dents on Riley wing and repainting 12 shillings'. Durrants, the butchers, paid £1 for signwriting in gold leaf on a van and what a big job repainting Mr. Allen's taxi must have been in 1929 when it cost £10. William's 'big break' came when local company Electrolux gave him the opportunity to quote for painting and signwriting their first six motorcycles and sidecars, which were the start of their

Electrolux remained a valued customer of W.Childs for over seventy years. In 1930, Bill's (he was always known as Bill) perception was proved right and he bought premises at 224 High Town Road, which were in fact retained after closure many decades later. Emily and Bill had already moved to Luton and were living in Winch Street but now moved to the new High Town Road address where John Alan was born in 1936. Number 224 was previously the property of the corn and seed merchant Thomas Davies, who was a relative of the Luton Girls Choir founder Arthur Davies.

As the motor vehicle population of the town increased, new buildings were erected and Bill built up his business with repair and finishing shops covering 12,000 sq.ft. In 1936 the buildings at 251, directly opposite the main site, were acquired and converted to a separate spray shop as the use of cellulose

The High Town Road yard in 1930 (DC)

service fleet. Dickinson & Adams were his competitor but William's successful quote was a few shillings cheaper than theirs. Shortly after, Electrolux bought twenty vans and once again his quote was successful, but these had to be painted, written and delivered one a day, with a head start of one week. The Electrolux contract involved painting the vans in dark blue and signwriting in gold leaf.

paints in the industry increased. Number 251 had been for some years where Frederick Cooper was a motor engineer and hirer of charabancs for private parties. During WW2, Bill turned to producing farm trailers and was subcontracted to paint aircraft fuel tanks and small items for the war effort. After the war the opportunity arose to purchase land adjoining 224 from Arthur Powdrill, which included the remnants of J. Bull's rope works. Further workshops were constructed for heavy vehicle repair and painting, part of the building work being completed by Johnson Fuller Ltd. The extra space allowed more vehicles to be dealt with at the same time and this space was centrally heated to provide the warm air that was essential for drying paints at the correct temperature. The oil-fired central heating system installed by R.S.Glyde of Guildford Street produced a quick heat build-up, important for achieving a fine finish. The Childs family firm was always self-contained and carried out all processes, including signwriting. The customer base had grown and represented a wide cross section of old and new Luton businesses and included, as well as Electrolux, some other larger companies like Skefko, Blue Circle Cement, H.C.Janes and Eastern Gas Since the early years Bill Childs had worked for the market gardeners of mid-Bedfordshire. He said "Some of our present customers among the market gardeners are people who have been dealing with us for generations. In the old days we made carts and trolleys for their grandfathers. They have known us since their childhood and now they come to us to paint their lorries."

Everyone who went to the Commercial Motor Show at London's Earls Court during the 1950s through to the 1970s admired the wonderful finishes applied to the vehicles on the stands. For years Commer Cars (subsequently Rootes, then Chrysler Dodge) sent their vehicles intended for exhibition to Childs for that special 'exhibition finish' to be applied. Each job took hundreds of hours, even the chassis and castings being prepared and painted to show standard. In 1968 the total cost of preparation and painting a Commer 8-ton chassis cab with twin rear axles, a Walk-Thru van, a 15 cwt Commer van including some modifications and a Commer Imp van came to £1,190. Their years of

Electrolux vans after signwriting in 1935 (DC)

Some of the staff in 1949 (DC)

experience in this field was used when Vauxhall Motors asked them to restore a 1927 Vauxhall for one of the Vice Presidents of General Motors. In fact, before the name Bedford was used, the first Chevrolet van produced at the Vauxhall factory in Luton was painted by Childs for The Luton News.

In 1961 a limited company with 24 employees was formed and Bill's two sons joined him as directors. Derrick had shown a talent for art and practiced signwriting whilst at school, earning pocket money at the age of 12 for writing car number plates. Before WW2 Percival Aircraft employed Derrick as a woodworker at Luton Airport, working on the fuselage and tail sections of the Proctor Trainer. He worked there for two years under a reserved occupation and during this time met his future wife Joan Champken who was a secretary there. In 1942 he was 'called-up' and joined REME, serving in the Normandy campaign and the army of occupation. His duties included repairing and rebuilding bulldozers and excavators and the repair of equipment in Caen Laundry after its damage. He rejoined his father in 1946. Younger son John joined the firm in 1957 after National Service, also in REME, and was married in 1961. Their sister Mary married and emigrated to the U.S.A. in 1945 and still lives in California. During the 1960s Derrick and John worked long hours spraying, painting and signwriting. When a large vehicle was hand varnished it meant an early start and a very late finish to the day, retaining the 'wet edge' so essential to a fine finish. In late 1961 Bill's health began to deteriorate and the following year he retired, enjoying his home in Old Bedford Road where he indulged his love of music. He died in 1970. Derrick and John continued in business for a further thirty-two years, assisted by Derrick's son David , born in 1959, who joined the company in 1975. David attended Luton Technical College, achieving both Institute of the Motor Industry qualifications and City & Guilds Full Technological Certification. Some of the craftsmen employed at Childs were happy to stay for many years, two throughout their working lives and a number of others gave over 25 years of service. Derrick's father-in-law Fred Champken also worked for the company for many years. In 1978 Derrick fulfilled a lifelong ambition to own a British sports car when he bought a 1957 Aston Martin DB2/4 which he and David restored in their spare time. It won many prizes at club and national events and still remains in the family. In 1993 W. Childs Ltd. was the

Examples of Childs' work for local companies. (DC)

first body shop in the area to achieve British Standards BS5750. During this period they were also listed as approved repairers for a large number of insurers and work providers. To achieve this they had invested in much of the latest repair technology, including the latest spot and MIG welding equipment, computerised paint-mixing and wheel alignment facilities together with computerised estimating and video imaging systems in the office. This brought more work, but the insurers were making extra conditions for the retention of their custom, including asking for free loan cars and also imposing restrictions on pricing. These pressures meant processing even more vehicles and made it difficult for a

company that was not prepared to compromise on quality, pressures that still confront most accident repair specialists to this day. Derrick died, aged 74, in 1995 and John continued working until his retirement in 1999. David remained running the company until 2002 when he decided there was no appreciable margin of profitability remaining within this sector of the trade. This highly regarded enterprise, which had been built up over the years on the basis of customer recommendations, high quality workmanship and personal service, closed after more than eighty years in Luton. Their location is now occupied by the Breachwood Repair Centre & Body Shop and the Calvin Smith Sign Company.

COSBY'S STORES

This is a story of New Town Street in Luton, the area of the town that the locals once called "The Borough". It was mostly rows of houses built back to back and generally intended for the industrious classes. Prior to the visit from the Government Inspector from the General Board of Health in the mid-nineteenth century, the area contained many houses in a constant damp state caused by surface drains. In New Town Street many houses had open cesspools and, although there was a well in the street, it was difficult to draw water, so none was drawn for flushing purposes.

Of course, the condemned housing of that time is no longer with us and this story of "The Borough" begins about 1930. Bert Cosby had married Sophie Maria Elizabeth in 1908 when they were 19. Both were Lutonians born in 1889 and they lived at number 6 Chase Street

where they used to sell from their front room which faced directly onto the pavement. Sophie, who was know to everyone as Liz, used to chop logs to sell as firewood and also scrub celery for resale, which was quite a chore. Liz churned her own ice cream and shaped it into bricks which Bert sold from a wooden hand barrow. Their hard work bore fruit, for on 18th August 1931 they had saved enough money to purchase, from Markyate resident Charles Cook, the general store a few doors away from their home on the corner with New Town Street, next to the "Sugar Loaf" public house, where numbers 110 and 112 cost them £500.

They recalled that at this time the shop displayed only one jar of sweets and one tin of snuff, so opening stock was taken on a sale-or-return basis from local wholesalers. They were successful with their general store which became the hub of the local community, providing more than a place to buy food and drink. The many advertising hoardings on the building tell us of Liptons tea and Lyons tea and cocoa, Colmans and Reckitts starch, Hudsons soap and Mansion polish, Wills Gold Flake cigarettes and the local Burgess mineral waters. In 1937 the decision was taken to

Nelson, the one-eyed family whippet, outside the original shop, c1930 (SCo)

(l to r) Bert and Liz Cosby, Cliff and Phyllis Taylor (SCo)

demolish the old premises and rebuild with a new shop and also with a new home above. Sadly Bert died in 1939 at the age of 50. Liz and Bert had three children and happily Phyllis their daughter was now old enough to join her mother in the shop. Together they ran the shop through the WW2 period of food rationing and coupons until Phyllis's husband Clifford Taylor returned from active service as a sergeant in the Royal Army Service Corps. They had married at St. Paul's Church in 1939 but they first met aged 13 when at Surrey Street School. Clifford, whose father was head gardener at the local hospital, had earlier worked for the Luton Gas Company, but now he joined the family firm.

For the next 25 years Liz, Phyllis and Cliff worked steadily increasing the turnover, Cliff driving a small van to make deliveries to their customers over a wider area, even to their 'posh customers' in Cutenhoe Road. They also opened for business on Sunday mornings and even on the morning of Christmas Day. The family lived in their new accommodation over the shop, now including the next generation of Shirley and Robert who can remember many of the products which were sold. Snuff, cigarettes and sweets were on sale and also Tincture of Rhubarb which it was understood would help settle the stomach. Lifebuoy, Lux and Pears soap and of course 'Persil Washes Whiter'. Camp coffee, Horlicks and Ovaltine which 'builds up brain, nerve and body'. Beechams Pills, Andrews Liver Salts and Bovril which 'prevents that sinking feeling'. They remember the huge sides of bacon, the circular cheddars in traditional cheesecloth, Hickmans delivering the daily bread for resale. Tomatoes from Pecks at Woburn Sands were displayed in the wooden bins outside on the pavement and also fresh locally grown vegetables from market gardener Harry Squires of Maulden.

In 1974, after 43 years, Cosby's Stores ceased to be in the Cosby family when, due to Phyllis's ill health and the long working hours, the shop was sold to Thomas Bee. Cliff took a job representing the Peter Keens Company, later worked in stores at Electrolux and died in 1982. Phyllis worked part-time in perfumery and fashions with Blundells and Debenhams and died in 2002. The King Do Chinese Takeaway occupies the premises now.

Bert Cosby (right) and helpers selling ice-cream bricks (SCo)

The rebuilt shop in 1937 (SCo)

E. DEACON

Named in memory of "The Iron Duke", Wellington Street was built in the mid nineteenth century on agricultural land. It was a brand new road between George Street and Stuart Street and was to become one of the busiest shopping streets in the town. It contained a shop which many friends have suggested I should try to include in this book and that is the emporium of Deacon's. However that has not proved to be as undemanding as most stories herein, for it transpires that the Deacon's were not outstanding at retaining family records.

Whilst always courteous and friendly, they would be best described as quiet, some say 'dreamy', and they certainly did not communicate with each other.

Edwin Deacon was born in Luton in 1845. His father, Timothy Deacon, was a member of one of the oldest families in the neighbourhood and a farmer. He was also a shopkeeper, carrier and coal dealer in Stuart Street. Timothy died in 1862 at the age of 54. Edwin was the founder of the business which was originally in the premises occupied by Messrs. Bird & Hudson, plait merchants, in Wellington Street and as a result of his trading capabilities Luton saw the gradual growth of his establishment. He commenced as a jeweller only and then expanded into the domain of fancy goods and china, taking

Edwin and Annie Deacon (JSq)

over other shops nearer George Street, the needlework and wool departments following. In 1889 Mr. Deacon found his existing premises inadequate and he built new commodious shops at 3,5 and 7 Wellington Street. He was also in business at 26 George Street and when this was closed no's 77 and 79 in George Street were opened, which meant that they had almost complete control of this prominent corner in the town's shopping centre. However Mrs H. Baker was resident for about 15 years in the corner premises between the Deacon shops. Her husband Richard had previously been a milliner at 10 Wellington Street and they were living at 10 Stockwood Crescent. She was a ladies' outfitter, selling millinery, flowers, feathers and straw hats and she gave special attention to wedding and mourning orders. When she retired in 1913, and Deacon's took the premises, their 'corner' was created and this was when the large, well-remembered public clock was placed on the first floor. Edwin lived with his wife Annie above number 9 Wellington Street, where he had a trapdoor placed in the floor directly above the cash till. From here he could espy the transactions in the shop below! They later moved to 'Normanclyde' which became 11 Dunstable Road, a large Victorian house which boasted a beautiful wooden staircase, all of which was destroyed when the new Post Office was built. Seven children were born to Edwin and Annie. They were Clarice, who was always known as Tess, Herbert, Arthur, Beatrice known as Bea, Olive known as Dolly, Verenia known as Ree and

Raymond who died in action at Gallipoli during WW1. Dolly and Tess both moved to Bournemouth on their marriages, Bea and Ree worked in the shops and Bert and Arthur were named in the company title of E. Deacon & Sons. Arthur, who was born in Luton in 1876, was to become the craftsman jeweller. He married Barbara Weatherhead in 1901 and lived at 13 Downs Road, where Barbara gave birth to twins, Marjorie and Eric. Marjorie was to marry Luton hat manufacturer Alec Staddon and their daughter Janet is still resident in Luton. Eric joined the family firm. One of Arthur's duties was clockwinding throughout the town, keeping Lutonians punctual at, among others, The Davis Gas Stove Company, the Co-Op Cocoa Works and the central Corn Exchange. He was a small man and able to negotiate the narrow passage up to the Corn Exchange clock. However, it stopped when he was unwell, for Eric, who was somewhat larger, was unable to squeeze through! In 1888 George Barley, Town Clerk, accepted Mr. Deacon's tender to deal with the Corporation's clocks and in 1894 William Austin wrote from the Clerk's Office in George Street West accepting his offer to look after "the clocks of the Workhouse, more especially the Boardroom clock, at a renumeration of 25/- per year, the contract to be determinable at the pleasure of the Board". In 1919, when the Town Hall was burned down, Marjorie, like many other town shop keepers, watched the blaze from an upstairs window.

Oliver, brother of Charles Farmbrough,

The Wellington Street shops (TGHobbs)

house furnisher of Park Square, worked for Deacon's for a short time. He, also being of slight stature, was able to include clockwinding for customers among his duties. He always enjoyed calling at The Larches in New Bedford Road, the home of brewer J. W. Green, to wind and correct his clocks. Before joining Deacon's, Oliver was, in 1900, apprenticed for five years to Walter Lester of Dunstable to learn "The Art of Watch, Clock & Jewellery repairing". His

indenture lists many things that he must do and "his Master faithfully serve and his secrets keep". In addition "he shall not contract Matrimony, nor play Cards or

Herbert (left) and Arthur Deacon (JSq)

The Wellington Street corner

Dice Tables or any other unlawful Games". He was paid "two shillings (10p) per week, three shillings in the next year and an increase of 1/6 per week each year afterward".

The large establishment of Deacons was always crowded with customers and window shoppers. Their stock varied from clothing to cutlery and from trunks to tie-pins. In 1908 ladies silver watches sold there for 10/- (50p) and gents' for 12/6 (62 1/2p). There were gold rings and brooches, gold pins for ties and scarfs, cruet stands and clocks from 1/6 (7 1/2p) to 7/6 (37 1/2p). Glass, china and fancy drapery departments were mainly at numbers 3 and 5 and they were agents for Goss china. Numbers 7 and 9 were for fancy goods and jewellery. There were also leather goods, toys, dolls, stationery, wools and earthenware on sale. All materials were stocked for embroidery, knitting and rugmaking, so in 1934 they held a special two-week demonstration of

"Weevella, the New Homecraft" which needed "no machines and no needles". At number 9 Arthur reigned supreme, for he loved watchmaking, indeed he was said by some to be brilliant in his work. Assistant Mr. William Dobbs, who lived at 17 Moor Street, may well be remembered, for he worked with the family for more than 78 years, saying when asked about retirement at the age of 92 that "he was thinking about it". Edwin was intimately associated with the history and growth of Luton commerce. His keen business aptitude resulted in the transformation of a small jeweller's shop into a large emporium enjoying a wide patronage. He was a clever jeweller and designer and was awarded a gold medal for designing in brass at the Hastings Exhibition of 1868. He was a member of the Chamber of Commerce, a Wesleyan and a Unionist in politics, but his broadmindedness and impartiality always came before party claims. He was one of the trustees of the Luton General Cemetery Company and also a director of the Luton Laundry. He was buried in the Rothesay Road General Cemetery following his death in 1917 at the age of 72, but the business continued to run successfully until after the death of his wife Annie in 1937. On her death the full conditions of Edwin's will became operative and his estate had to be divided into fifteen parts between his seven children, in unequal shares according to their circumstances. This meant the disposal of the properties, and all that remained was number 9 Wellington Street from which Arthur continued with his son Eric. Because Arthur and Eric were craftsmen rather than businessmen or accountants, the business ran down and in 1950 the decision was taken to move into smaller and less costly premises at 65 Stuart Street. However, a few years after that, Eric left for other employment simply because the business could not support the two of them. Arthur carried on alone for a while, but the business was unfortunately not sustainable in Stuart Street and there was no alternative to closure. This is where the very well remembered Luton name of Deacon ended its life.

For many years the prominent corner premises became Saxone Shoes, later Omni and is now the local branch of the Nationwide Building Society. A plaque on their premises records that in 1998 the Luton Borough Council presented them with the Luton Design Award for the restoration and refurbishment of the building. Further up Wellington Street, no.5 is now estate agents John Williams & Co., No.7 became N. Gold & Sons and is now Response Personnel Ltd. Number 9 was taken over by Zip French Cleaners and is now Anglian Home Improvements. Around the corner in George Street no.79 was to become Stones Fashions and is now part of British Home Stores. In Stuart Street no.65 changed into Parisienne Cleaners and is now part of the Stuart Street flyover.

M. FELSON

East-Enders....that's the local Felson family! Maurice was born in Whitechapel in 1896 of Polish parents. He was a market trader from an early age, selling toiletries in the London markets. He began to travel in our direction after he had found himself a Carving Knife (wife, to you and me) when, in 1927, he married Rachel Cohen whose parents were Russian. Then, together with fellow trader Cyril Harris, he began selling on the open market at St.Albans. Cyril sold stockings, ladies' separates and children's clothing whilst Maurice was selling toiletries as before. In 1929 he chose to move with his family to Luton and live first at 66 Kingston Road. Their son Martin is a Londoner, for he was also born in Whitechapel only three weeks before their move to Luton. Martin attended Luton Modern School but his father decided that he would leave at 14 as he wanted him to join the family business. Previously, in 1925, the Plait Halls in Cheapside and Waller Street in Luton had come to the end of their useful life and the market moved in, to be under cover for the first time. A few years later Maurice and Rachel took stalls here and traded successfully on their individual stands for many years. Rachel's stall in the centre aisle was always busy, as she sold mouthwatering chocolates and ice cream and also cigarettes. Maurice had a stall adjacent to the outer wall, from which he continued to sell toiletries for both men and women and also added disinfectants. Promoted strongly by Denis Compton advertisements, 'Brylcreem', the original hairdressing for men, sold well but was 'like gold dust and reserved for regular customers' during the war when it was in short supply. Everything of course was offered at a 'good and fair price'. Martin was helping now and expanded sales into hairdressing products. Some supplies came from hairdressers' sundriesman John Maclaren in Chapel Street, who was able to supply them with the trade version of the retail products ColorGlo and Inecto. Ladies' hairdressers in the town didn't like this as Felson's were making life difficult for them by selling direct to the public, but this led to

Maurice Felson (MF)

Martin Felson at his market stall, 1991 (MF)

the basis for a lucrative 'home-hairdressing' business. Their customers were now able to use the same lower priced products at home as were being used in the professional salons.

So many have happy memories of the old covered market and Martin particularly recalls those that were trading near to him. He remembers Isenberg's Cut Shop, Nellie and Vic Ayres who had two stalls selling antiques and what today we would call collectables, and Albert Moule's Tea Shop where Martin used to buy jugs of tea for 6d. until on one visit he saw a tea-towel being used as a handkerchief! He also recalls seeing a wedding group there, well dressed and wearing carnations, eating their wedding breakfast of pork pies! On one side of Felson's toiletries stall was Rita Mayover, later Mrs. Rita Navarre, who sold costume jewellery and on the other side was Jim Holmes, the cutler and tool dealer. Another of Martin's memories involves saccharines. During the war he would make weekly train journeys to Stoke Newington in London where, for his father, he would visit a manufacturing chemist. He would bring sacks of these back to Luton, each containing tens of thousands of the tablets. Maurice employed two ladies who used their kitchen tables to repack them into small quantities for resale. Felson's did a roaring trade in saccharines!

Just before WW2, during which he was an air-raid warden, Maurice bought the lease on 57 George Street which had previously been occupied by H.A.Leon & Co. This was a very, very small shop, squeezed between the National Provincial Bank and the Pearl Assurance Company. It measured (and still does) about 9ft by 7ft, it was a kiosk really. Even in that small space it included a stairway which customers climbed to the hairdresser's salon on the floor above. It was called Maison Rachelle but in 1948 Sid and Susie Gold took it over, renaming it George's Salon. After National Service with the RAF, Martin joined his mother in the George Street kiosk, she having given up her sweetshop market stall to be here. In 1953 Martin found a Duchess of Fife (again, a wife to you and me) when he married Barbara Harris from Harcourt Street at the Luton Synagogue in Bury Park Road (originally the Empire Cinema and now the Islamic Centre). A coincidence is that Barbara was also born in Whitechapel and even in the same nursing home. They had met when Martin offered to walk Barbara home after a dance at Luton Town Hall. It was Barbara's 16th birthday. They lived at first in Marlborough Road, then both Old and New Bedford Roads before settling in Montrose Avenue. They were blessed with three children, Romaine, Steven and Adele and now six grandchildren and celebrated their Golden Wedding in 2003.

In 1954, Rachel died at the age of only 47, just one year after Martin and Barbara were married. Sadly Martin's younger brother John also died, at the age of only 21. This meant that Maurice had to look after the George Street kiosk whilst Martin took over the market stall, until the time came for the demolition of the covered market and the historic Plait Halls, making space for the Arndale Centre. In January 1972 Martin was able to move with many of his fellow market traders into the new covered market

within the new shopping centre, taking units 9 and 10. Martin's friend John Edelnand was a great help in fitting out the new stall with display cabinets at the rear of the unit. John would soon be opening his own new shop, Edma Jewellers, just along the mall. Close to Martin's new stall was Joe Sherman who continued his many years in the market, simply specialising in men's socks. Barbara was always ready to help Martin on their stall when needed and her sister Shirley Feld was also behind the counter for many years.

Maurice had remarried two years after Rachel's death but both he and his second wife died within two months of each other in 1977. Martin Felson successfully traded in the Arndale Centre Market Hall for another seventeen years, only selling his flourishing and popular business in September 1998 when retirement beckoned. It continues under the name of L & R Supplies. Nowadays, Martin enjoys the company of good friends who share his enthusiasm for short-mat bowling, and Barbara is busy teaching Spanish to friends in the U3A. She has given twelve years service to the WRVS delivering meals-on-wheels, is a volunteer in the Luton Crown Court and also a Member of the Luton Council of Faith.

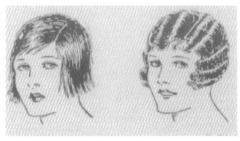

THE FIFTY SHILLING TAILORS

In Luton number 47 George Street was, for something like seventy years, home to outfitters for both ladies and gentlemen. From the turn of the twentieth century it was J. Hepworth & Sons who set the fashion, but after 1935 Sir Henry Price took control. First in his own name as Price's Tailors, but in 1938 whilst he was Company Chairman, the name was changed to that which would become nationally famous … The Fifty Shilling Tailors. Indeed he became known personally as The Fifty Shilling Tailor. Originally Leeds based, Sir Henry and Lady Eve made their fortune making off-the-peg suits, moving in 1938 into Wakehurst Palace in West Sussex where a garden there is still named after him. He is well-remembered in horticultural circles by the various plants which bear his and his wife's names. For many years it was indeed possible to buy a fashionable well-cut suit or costume for fifty shillings – two pounds ten shillings (£2.50)!! The company name remained, although through the years the prices obviously increased. When the window price was £5.19s.6d customers were pressured to buy at £7.19s.6d or £9.19s.6d for a better quality cloth. The photographs I took of the George Street branch about 1950

47 George Street in 1950

show that a made-to-measure suit could be purchased for £6.19s.6d. My girl friend at the time (and wife to be) is viewing the window on the right.

The shop had large display windows with a walkway around a central window to the entrance and there were two sales floors. The windows were not dressed by the staff, but by a circuit team of two or three who would call once a month to renew the display, always commencing with clean white paper on the floor of each window. Staff could not sell from the windows because the suits were only "shells", having no linings or pockets. Made-to-measure clothing occupied the ground floor where there were large racks displaying the rolls of material available, a separate display of raincoats, a fitting room and the cashier's desk that was occupied for many years by Muriel Horton. The Branch Manager at this time was Roland Moss. Jack Cornish was in charge of made-to-measure and once you set foot inside his department you were very unlikely to get out without making a purchase or, at the very least, leaving a half-crown deposit on a raincoat which you were probably unsure you really needed. Selling was on a commission basis, the sales pitch was very high pressure and Jack was a master at convincing people that they really did need that raincoat.

A long flight of stairs led to the first floor, with another fitting room for the ready-to-wear department for suits, raincoats and overcoats. Danny Heckan was in charge of this floor. He was always immaculately dressed in a well-pressed suit, stiff white collar, gleaming shoes and, when he went out, always a grey homburg hat. There was a staff refreshment room but it was in the dark, damp and unheated basement. Jack Cornish was born in Norwich and worked with The Fifty Shilling Tailors in his home city, followed by Great Yarmouth, Newbury, Aylesbury and Ilkeston before coming to

The good display of suits, 1950

Jack Cornish and John Robson.

made-to-measure department under Jack Cornish who taught me all there was to know about measuring people, not only gentlemen but ladies as well, as we used to do a lot of ladies' costumes. Jack was a very good teacher and made me watch each time he measured someone and would say things like 'DRS Half Inch' or 'HB One Inch'. This code was his own, DRS meaning 'drop right shoulder' for if person is right handed his or her shoulder is lower than the left. HB meant the customer had a slight hump back but he always used the code so as not to offend. After a while he let me measure customers for a suit under his supervision and he always checked each measurement so that there was no mistake. It was at this time at the tender age of 16, that I think I had the most embarrassing moment of my life. Jack and the Manager were not available and a very large frumpish woman wanted a costume made and it was down to me to measure her. After she had picked out the material she wanted I began the task of measuring her. This involved her holding one end of the tape measure and me running round with my end of the tape, as my arms were not long enough to

the Luton branch in 1952. Jack still lives in Luton and, at the age of 86, has helped with these memories.

My brother-in-law, John Robson, joined The Fifty Shilling Tailors in 1952 at the weekly salary of £3.00 following an interview which lasted all of ten minutes. He has many memories of his time there and recalls some here. "Quite often a customer purchasing a ready made suit would need to have it altered in some way and it was my job to take these suits round to the tailor Mr. Tresman in Guildford Street. It was no easy task walking through the town with perhaps six or seven suits and then bring back those he had completed. If he was in a bad mood he would jabber on at me in Yiddish. After spending some months in the ready-to wear section, I moved to the

go round her. So far, so good, but then disaster struck. She decided she would have a pair of slacks made from the same material so that she would have a costume and a trouser suit. So what, you might ask! The way to measure a lady's inside leg is as follows … (1) measure waist … (2) measure the outside leg from waist to shoe…. (3) sit the customer on a chair and measure from waist to seat of chair …. (4) deduct measurement at 3 from outside leg measurement at 2 …. no problem so far, but when I asked the lady to sit on the chair so that I could measure from waist to chair she says "I want none of this nonsense, do it properly young man!" and with this she pulls her skirt right up to the waist, spreads her legs and says "Get on with it!" Red bloomers and

whalebone corsets have given me the shakes ever since!" It was in 1953 that we arrived at the shop one day to find that we were now John Collier. Remember? "John Collier, John Collier, the Window to Watch". John left John Collier in that year to join Webb Brothers on the corner of George Street and Bute Street at an increased salary of £7.00 a week. He eventually went on to manage a number of Woolworth Stores, finally at Taunton and is now retired in Somerset.

In the years that followed the end of WW2 the most popular size for an off-the-peg suit was 38" chest and 30" waist. Today Lewis Carroll's walrus would still weep "for those of the largest size", for now it is 42" chest and 34" waist.

FISHERS

The butcher's window display is that which changes most quickly. Always their fresh show of meats are quickly refilled once a piece has been sold. Introduced to improve hygiene, byelaws now prevent meat on hooks being displayed outside the shop, it nowadays having to be enclosed in polythene. The magnificent displays of yesteryear may be remembered by those of us who can recall the Luton butcher's shops of the Fisher family.

About 1903 Arthur Edmund Fisher opened his first shop at 25 George Street, next to Boots Cash Chemists which was on the corner with Chapel Street. This remained head-office but there were also branches opened at 52 High Town Road, at 223 Dunstable Road between Beech and Oak Roads, and at 644 Hitchin Road in Stopsley. Out of town they traded in Watford and Dunstable. They were quality wholesale and retail butchers, poulterers and purveyors of cooked meats. To the rear of the George Street shop was the slaughterhouse and also the sausage house where, obviously, sausages were produced for all the branches. Faggots were prepared here and cooked for them by the White Rose Catering Co. The slaughterhouse was owned by the family and was one of about 12,000 private slaughterhouses known to exist in this country before WW2. The company stockyard was about 200yds away up

25 George Street in 1918 (SC)

Chapel Street, near where the Stuart Street flyover is today. Animals for slaughter were herded down Chapel Street from here and quite often rebelled at the idea. Sheep were known to run in to Eveling's shop and be herded out through another door. On one occasion a ram, having seen its reflection in Partridge's window, stormed through their doorway and wrecked many bicycles which were on display inside.

Stanley Clark, who lives in Lower Woodside, spent fifty years in the Luton

The Wartime Savings Campaign outside Fisher's

butchery trade working for Fisher's, Frost's, Bishop's and the Co-Op. Born in Dagenham, evacuated to Gloucestershire, then to Manor Road in Luton, he attended Surrey Street School and at first joined Hayward-Tyler as a moulder. His

father had worked with Fisher's and Stan joined them when he was 15 years old. It was a typical butcher's shop of that time with sawdust on the floor and with big wooden meat-chopping blocks. Some butchers used to display a sign 'No Smoking or Expectorating'. I always wondered what that meant. Stan's wartime memories are of the weekly ration of 2/- of meat and 6d worth of corned beef and, if a customer was lucky, some offal or a couple of sausages or some dripping. Stan recalls that, during rationing, staff were encouraged to gain as many registered customers as they could, for they could earn an extra 6d for each ration book registered with Fisher's. One of his jobs as a junior was to hose down the display of meat if it had been dirtied by the passing buses when they drove through the gutters near the shopfront! The Ministry of Food controlled prices during the war and Stan believes they were about 3/6 lb for rump steak, 2/- lb for a joint of beef and 1/- lb for stewing steak.

Arthur Fisher lived in Hart Lane for many years, at Ingleside, before numbering had taken place, and eventually retired to Torquay. His son Morton, who lived in a suite of rooms at the George Hotel, became managing

25 George Street in 1950 (SC)

director at this time. In 1967 the Fisher family sold the last of their business interests in Luton, the George Hotel, which they had owned for forty years. 'The Saturday Telegraph' believed the price paid by Littlewoods was in the region of £750,000. Fisher's the butchers served the people of Luton for about sixty years, changing to a self-service shop in George Street for a short time before final closure. It was vacant for some years and then used by the Luton Consumer Advice Centre. Gent's tailor Geoff Souster traded from there and now the building is noticeably colourful as Jean's Flower Shop.

Geere and Co., Ltd
Sculptors and Masons

It was way back in 1898 that Matthew Geere set up Geere & Co. at 233 Dunstable Road, Luton, between Oak and Ash Roads and next to the Primitive Methodist Church from whom he leased the building. Before this Matthew, who

Matthew Geere, aged 71, in 1947 (WG)

was born in 1876, lived in Chatham where both his father and his grandfather before him had been masons working in the building industry. He married Muriel Cudmore and it was a second marriage for them both. Matthew's first wife had died of consumption and Muriel's first husband had died from the effects of the Great War. Muriel was fourteen years younger than Matthew. They had three sons, Harry, Fred and George and also Joseph from Muriel's first marriage.

In 1897, at the age of 21, Matthew came to Luton and lived for a short time at 60 Rothesay Road, taking a job as journeyman mason with local stonemasons Low Giddings. However, determined to move forward on his own, in the following year he started his own business as a sculptor and monumental mason, using a horse and cart to deliver his work where it was required. This was at first from Cromwell Road and later in Dunstable Road. Many of the Geere family moved to Bedfordshire from Chatham at this time and Matthew and his wife set up home at 'Burnside' in Wilstead. Business prospered under Matthew's enthusiastic direction, for in only five years he was advertising that he had nearly a hundred memorials in stock. Arthur Wing, known to all as Bill, was taken on as an apprentice when a young boy and was the only apprentice ever to be retained. He became highly skilled and, apart from war service in Burma, stayed with the Geere family for most of his life, all of 70 years. Harry, Fred and George joined their father, learned and became proficient in the techniques of

233 Dunstable Road,1930, with the Chevrolet lorry (WG)

masonry and became equal directors of the company. Joseph also entered with them as their traveller. Marble was imported into Luton in 20-ton container loads from Carrara in Tuscany, north-west Italy. Famous for its white marble which has been worked since Roman times, it was a favourite material of Michelangelo. Pre-cast concrete came from Chiltern Concrete Products in Barton-le-Clay and granite was supplied by Galloway Granite Works from Newton Stewart in Scotland and later imported from China. At one time Geere & Co. had branches in Bedford, St. Albans, Harpenden, Northampton and Rushden.

At the commencement of the hostilities of WW2, their 30-cwt Chevrolet lorry was commandeered by the government for use in the war effort and was not seen again. During this time deliveries were made using a pony and trap. Matthew had retired in 1936 at the ago of 60, but returned to work for the duration of the war. In peacetime the old buildings were demolished and the memorial of the angel playing her trumpet, which had been so admired over the years, lost her place in the forecourt. A more modern structure was built and business went from strength to strength. In 1952 their success allowed them to acquire the old-established business of Hitchin monumental masons, James Pepper & Co. in Walsworth Road. Many years earlier, comedian Bob Hope's father and uncle had worked there. Following this acquisition, George and Fred were based at Hitchin whilst Harry and Joseph looked after the Luton premises. Matthew, the founder, died in 1954, aged 78.

The rebuilt premises, c1955 (WG)

Bill Wing at work, c1970 (WG)

For 99 years, the Geeres provided an essential service to the local community, meeting all the needs of individuals who wished to commemorate their loved ones. Harry said "You need to be able to listen to the customer, interpret their ideas and let them decide what they want. In that I think we succeeded." The three brothers certainly went to a lot of trouble to satisfy all the ethnic groups in our area, making memorials in any language. They were all proud that the business stayed in the family for so many years. Harry retired in 1992 and died two years later. His widow, Winnie, still lives in Luton. Fred retired to the Bedfordshire village of Gravenhurst and died in 2001. His widow, Maisie, still lives there. The only descendent in the family was Harry's daughter Vicky who became a director for seven years. However George sold the company in 1997 and still enjoys retirement with his wife Kreena in nearby Clophill. Geere & Co., the long-established firm of high class sculptors and monumental masons, producing memorials of beauty and design, is no longer in their hands. It is now owned by a London company who retain the valued name.

'CURLY' GILBERT

Meet Curly Gilbert, a warm-hearted cheerful man who earned this jocular name when he lost most of his hair in his early twenties. But first read about his father, William Gilbert, who was born on the upper floor of the stable block in the grounds of Frank Scargill's residence which we now know as Wardown Park. His father, Curly's grandfather, was head groom. William, who later lived at 11 New Street, became a horse dealer in Chapel Street. He was able to tell many stories of his life with horses and how he used to race them up New Street, around the horse trough and back again. When selling a horse it was customary to improve its appearance by placing holly on the ground if it was prone to not walking straight and, if it limped a little on one leg, a sharp kick on the other leg would quickly mask this frailty. Tragically he died at the age of 42, having succumbed to pneumonia. It was believed he became ill whilst he was a carriage-driver for the Royal Mail.

William and his wife Ellen had four children, three girls and William Edward, Curly to us, who was born in 1909. Schooling was at the Chapel Street schools where he was in the same class as Billy Edwards who was later to become Mayor of Luton. Curly joined the Old Boys Association and gained himself a job as errand boy at C. H. Horwood's game, poultry and fishmonger's shop at 28 Chapel Street. The photograph of the shop with this story shows that they are offering rabbits at 1/6 and 1/8. One of Curly's duties was carrying blocks of ice on his bicycle up to the big house in Stockwood Park. He had inherited his father's love of horses and so was happy to make deliveries for a local hat manufacturer, using their horse and cart. In 1929, when he was 20, Curly married Lucy Hill at St. Paul's Church

Errand boy 'Curly' at Horwood's Chapel Street shop, 1924 (DG)

and set up home at 71 Chase Street, later moving to Cowper Street. He was also a keen motor-cyclist at this time. In his early thirties he joined the trade which was to remain with him for the rest of his life. His sister Emily had married Fred Parsons and they lived in Farley Hill. Fred was a fruiterer and greengrocer in the local indoor market and also had a shop at 67 Chapel Street which Emily looked after. This was next to the United Counties Omnibus Company garage. It later became a Shell station and its space is now occupied by Kwik-Fit. Curly joined Fred and learned the business of supplying the people of Luton with the freshest produce. In a few years, as the country went to war, Curly left his job to become a full-time firefighter with the Auxilliary Fire Service. Originally based in Oxen Road, he later became a Leading Fireman at the Vauxhall Sub-Station and attended many of the big London blitzes.

'Curly' Gilbert

In peacetime Curly at first worked for the hauliers Houghton & Armitage in Guildford Street, but soon returned to his chosen trade and rejoined Fred Parsons. Three times a week he travelled from Luton at 4.30 am to Covent Garden in London. The freshest, greenest, heartiest vegetables were brought back for sale and, with restrictions still in effect, they held the sole permit for selling cherries in Luton. Bananas and other fruit were returning to the counter and in those days the oranges were individually wrapped in tissue. Potatoes were purchased locally from Alf Horne's market garden in Maulden.

67 Chapel Street in 1959

Emily and Fred sold their Chapel Street shop to Mr. Rayment but in 1959 Curly bought it back into the family when he opened up in his own name at number 67. His wife Lucy was also called in to help on occasions, as were their three children, Rita, Sheila and Derrick. He was proud of his window displays which changed with the seasons and the weather, always using the freshest produce. The hard vegetables formed the base, for they could stay in place for a few days. Apples, pears and oranges came next and on the top were the more sensitive fruit which would be changed many times during the day. Curly's years 'on his own' were successful, for he had acquired an intimate knowledge of his trade. He retired in 1964, enjoying motor-cycling and, still retaining his interest in the earlier form of riding, he kept two ponies in Cyril Brown's paddock at Pepperstock. He died in 1978.

It would be remiss not to devote the final paragraph to Curly's alternative life. He was a Master-of-Ceremonies, a Compere and a children's entertainer, singing at the piano. Posters announcing 'Curly Gilbert's Variety Show' were everywhere and they raised hundreds of pounds for local charities such as The Luton Boys' Club, The Luton Band, The Luton Gardens Association and also old people's groups. In 1962 his biggest success was persuading the celebrated concert pianist Sir Francis Cassell, whose home was at Putteridge Bury, to give a half-hour recital during his three-hour show in the Community Centre. It is said 'Variety is the Spice of Life, That gives it All its Flavour'. I am confident that Curly knew that.

'Curly' entertaining

E. A. GREEN,

Bookseller, Newsagent & Stationer

News!… Queen Victoria used the word as a plural, "The news from Austria are very sad and make one very anxious", but it is now almost always regarded as singular, "The news is very pleasing". In April 1975 the Marquess of Tavistock told the Luton and Dunstable branch of the National Federation of Retail Newsagents that they were an important part of Britain's national heritage. He said " This is probably the first shop many of us go into as a child. A few moments in a local newsagent's can tell one an immense amount about a town." Enough of the reference books but more news, for it formed an important part of the life of the founder of one of Luton's most remembered newsagents, E.A.Green.

Ebeneezer Albert Green was born at 73 Cardigan Street, Luton in 1895. His father worked for the Post Office in Luton and Ebeneezer attended the school in Waller Street and left, as was usual, at the age of 14. He also left home and worked for the Post Office in Buckingham where he lived in 'digs' and cycled home to Luton at weekends. World War I broke out when he was 19 and he joined the armed services. On his 21st birthday he was serving at Ypres, scene of some of the bitterest fighting. After the war he was employed by the Western Union Cable Company in London. However, the reason for this story being in this book commenced in 1924 when, with a £100 loan from his father, he became a partner

Ebeneezer 'Bert' Green

of Albert Nicholls who had his cycle shop at 21A New Bedford Road, Luton, but it traded as a newsagent's from this time. This shop however had only one more year successful trading when in 1927 the partnership was amicably dissolved and it became the newsagent's, bookseller's and stationer's that most of us can recall. Two years later, together with his parents who had by now moved to Hazelbury Crescent, Bert (for this is how everyone knew Ebeneezer) opened their second shop at 228 Biscot Road, moving once again, this time to live above the shop. For in this year Bert married, but sadly his wife died two years later. In 1930 Eva

Mary Bellman from Dale Road, Bedford had a job lined up with a Luton firm but was not successful in gaining it. She then heard that Mr Green needed another assistant, applied and was employed at the shop in New Bedford Road. Two years later, in 1932, Bert and Eva were married in Luton and their son Michael was born one year later. At this time Bert became President of the Luton Newsagents' Association. He was also easily recognized in Luton when driving his 1936 Chevrolet motor car.

The two shops prospered, selling a vast range of products. There were birthday, wedding, comic, visiting and post-cards. Bibles and Prayer Books. English Hymnals and Methodist Hymn Books. Children's books and School prizes. Technical books, drawing instruments and Faber Castell slide rules. Burnham, Swan and Waterman fountain pens and propelling pencils. Fashions and patterns. Cigarettes and tobacco and 'Warden Parchment' stationery. There were over a thousand novels in stock and a lending library in both branches which cost members 2d a week. Books for resale were purchased in London and delivered to Luton by train the following morning. Finally of course there was the daily news, all the national and local newspapers which were on display outside the shop with billboards all around declaring the news headlines of

Green's shop by the lamp-post in New Bedford Road (MG)

Inside the shop with (l to r) Bert, Eva and Elsie Cook in 1928 (MG)

the day. Remember The Daily Sketch or The News Chronicle? Maybe you were buying Chicks Own, Chums or Little Folks! I can remember looking forward to going into Green's each month when it was time to buy my Meccano Magazine. From 6.30 am each morning twelve delivery boys were busy sorting the newspapers and six hundred houses had their newspapers delivered to their doors for which Green's charged them an extra penny each week. The Luton Liberal Club in Manchester Street also received daily delivery, Bert was a member here and also of the Lansdowne Club. There were twenty other shops in Luton and surrounding towns which bore the name of Green's News but these belonged to Bill Green who was not related to Bert and his family. The New Bedford Road shop was only single storey because the

bridge carrying the Luton, Dunstable and Welwyn Railway was angled across where a second floor could have been. This bridge for many years displayed in large white letters "Thursday is Newsday", for then The Luton News was published on that day. It took Green's staff over an hour to sort The Luton News every Wednesday evening ready for Thursday delivery. Flooding into the premises was a major problem in the 1920s and 30s when the road under the bridge could be overwhelmed during a downpour. Despite this the shop had no water mains and no toilet! When it was necessary staff would run to the Co-Op chemists shop next door and use theirs! Just before WW2, renumbering of this road meant that Green's became number 25. During the war Bert was an air-raid warden based at The Palace Cinema in nearby Mill Street, where from the roof of the building they watched for German bombers every Thursday night, armed with a stirrup pump, a shovel and a bucket of sand. Burglaries were frequent and in 1964 a passing lorry lost a wheel which crashed through the shop window.

Michael Green married Leighton Buzzard girl Anne Lymbery in 1960 and they lived at 9 Black Swan Lane where they were able to indulge their love of horses, stabling them in garages on the premises. Michael worked at the Biscot Road shop with his mother Eva. Here, a Mr. Smith was a newspaper 'boy' until the age of 85! Eva's brother, Fred Bellman, worked in the town shop. In 1964 the New Bedford Road shop was sold to another local stationer's, Staddons, who then moved this trade to their Wellington Street shop when two years later, the local Council demolished both Green's

shop and the next door Co-Op chemists. This was to assist the road widening at that point, but to this date it has not happened and retirement flats now occupy the site. Michael was to continue and prosper in Biscot Road, in 1964 introducing the sale of tropical and cold water fish into the rear of the building. This was a personal interest of Michael's as a member of the Luton Aquarists' Society which saw him importing fish from Singapore for resale in Luton. He finally sold the business in 1991, ending more than sixty years of the respected name of Green's in the world of news in Luton. Anne and Michael are retired and still living in Luton when not indulging in their favourite pastime of holiday cruising. Ebeneezer 'Bert' Green had died in 1977 at the age of 84. He had never retired, ending his life in his shop… certainly, that was news!

Bert and his father outside the Biscot Road shop in 1927 (MG)

Hawkins Shoe Repairs

It is said that Crispin, a Roman, went to France to further Christianity and wholly maintained himself by making and mending shoes. He is now recognized as the patron saint of shoemakers and, following his lead, the local Hawkins family also wholly maintained themselves in the same way, by making and mending shoes.

Henry Hawkins was born in 1881 and lived with his mother Mary at 16 Henry Street in Luton. Leaving school at an early age, as was the norm in those days, he was apprenticed for five years to boot makers H. Lawson & Son in Manchester Street. At the age of only 20 he set up his own cobbler's shop on the ground floor of his Henry Street house. In those days the cobbler was often referred to as the snob. It became a busy and quite colourful little

Henry at the Henry Street shop in 1910 (DH)

shop with ladies' shoes being soled and heeled for 1/6 (7 1/2p) and gentlemen's costing a little more at 2/6 (12 1/2p). One step up over the stone doorstep and you were in the shop, which was always filled with that distinctive smell of leather. The entire walls were papered with large advertising posters for Redfern's and Phillip's rubber soles and heels, Blakeys segs and Cherry Blossom polishes. Henry would stand working at his bench in the window, his mouth full of brads as he hammered away at his shoes. The shelves were full of lasts, the steel models on which the shoes were made and repaired. On the pavement outside the shop stood rolls of leather, these being known in the trade as 'bends'. One bend was roughly half a cow, so one cow = two bends!

Dennis Hawkins (DH)

Henry married Lizzie Hammett in 1905 and they had four children, Reginald, Eva, Edna and Dennis. Being talented in the 'gentle craft' of shoe making he was able to provide footwear for them all. With a growing family they moved house to Cambridge Street in 1918 and then to Denbigh Road in 1924, although still keeping the business running in Henry Street. Son Reginald joined his father on leaving school, learning the trade from Henry. In 1933, at the age of 26, Reg had a new shop purpose-built at 30 Tudor Road and set up a shoe repair business of his own. He later married Vera and they had two daughters. This business flourished over the years until ill health forced him to retire in 1984 at the age of 77 and he died two years later. These premises are now occupied by O. C. Bespoke Tailor

When Reginald left his father's shop, younger son Dennis, then 14, left school and he too joined Henry to learn the trade. Part of his job on Monday mornings was to call at customers' homes to collect shoes for repair and to return them later, what a service! Dennis joined the armed forces in 1939 and was one of the many who landed in Normandy on D-Day plus One. During his wartime absence his cousin Alec helped keep the business running. On his return to 'civvy street' in 1946 Dennis gradually took over the running of the Henry Street shop and in 1948 married Joan Cain at St. Mary's Church. They set up home in Austin Road where they had two daughters Rose-Marie and Marian. An unusual occurrence in Joan and Dennis's life is

The Roman Road shop. (DH)

that they were both born in the same house in Cambridge Street, for the Cain family moved in as the Hawkins family were moving out.

The changing face of Luton reached out to Henry Street when it was demolished in 1964 and Power Court and adjacent factories were planned for that area. After 63 years of trading in the old premises, Dennis opened up in a bright new modern shop at 88 Roman Road on a busy parade of shops which also offered a grocer, a fruiterer and a wine merchant. Henry had by this time retired and lived just long enough to see Dennis established and trading as 'Shoecraft'. Repairing was the main business of the

day along with sales of slippers, plimsolls, baseball boots, wellingtons and sundry leather goods. Supplies of leather came from merchants A.E.Fountain of 57 Hibbert Street. Dennis's collection of old sewing machines and artefacts was quite unique as the shoe repair trade gradually faded and 'heel bars' replaced them in shopping centres. Shoecraft was one of the very few cobbler's shops where hand stitched soles remained something of a speciality. Joan and Dennis moved house to Toddington in 1977 but Dennis carried on the business in the Roman Road shop until his retirement in 1984. The shop is now a greengrocer's and fruiterer's.

A. J. Hodge

This is the story of Lutonian Albert Hodge, who during his 89 years became a central part of cycle history in the making. Indeed he was one of the leading lightweight cycle manufacturers in the country.

Albert John Hodge was born in Luton on 15th July 1877. He was the youngest son of George and Elizabeth Hodge who lived in Old Bedford Road. George was a bricklayer by trade and was 33 years old when Albert arrived, the last of his six children. He was christened John Albert but was always called Albert and in later years was known to everyone as "Pop". Albert grew up in Luton with his two brothers and three sisters and there is no doubt that he became fascinated with cycles. Particularly as at that time they were a new and exciting form of transport. It is almost certain that his keen eye observed many improvements that could be made to those early models and perhaps it was then that the seeds were sown for his lifetime involvement with cycles.

In 1898, at the age of 21, Albert married 22 year old Sarah Elizabeth Holyoak who came from a well-known Luton family. The ceremony was at Shoreditch in East London and it is likely that they moved to live in Wood Green,

Albert and Elizabeth with their family in 1920 (CH)

London, because his grandfather lived there and was landlord of a local public house. Seven years later Albert opened his first shop in White Hart Lane, Wood Green, which was rented for one pound a week. The premises included a shop fronting the street with a workshop at the rear. There was living accommodation above, for the family now included three children. Albert's full time employment was with Waterlow Brothers & Layton, the security printers, where he was responsible for work on country bank notes which were used by small independent banks who were authorised to issue their own paper money. While he was doing this, the responsibility for running the cycle shop was with his wife and eldest daughter. They sold spares and accessories together with their own frames. During the evenings Albert would build these frames and also carry out repairs. Right from this very first shop, all of Albert Hodge's frames were sold under the name of "Holly Cycles", this having been derived from his wife's maiden name. A number of moves were made in the following years, with shops and accommodation being taken in Wood Green, Tottenham, Upper Norwood and even Southend. Elizabeth continued to run the shops, adding cylinder records for phonographs to their sales. During Christmas Eve of 1909 nearly seven hundred cylinder records were sold at 1/- (5p) each. Albert Hodge was becoming well known as a cycle frame builder and his shop became a meeting place for club cyclists in the area. During the years 1902-1914 some of the greatest riders of the time used his frames, one gaining fourth place in the gruelling 192 mile event in the 1912 Swedish Olympics. Hodge tandems were also successfully used in record attempts.

With the end of the Great War, many of the club cyclists returned and the demand for lightweight cycles once more grew and Albert was able to work full time in his cycle business. Working alongside him was his 16 year old son John, now known to all as "Holly" Hodge. Advertisements for Holly Cycles appeared both locally and nationally and the name was also painted onto the Tottenham Palace Music Hall safety curtain in large red lettering. The Little Red Holly cycle was costing £14/14/0 at this time and the

'Pop' Hodge in his Princess Street workshop, c1952 (CH)

tandem was £26/10/0. During 1930 Albert and Elizabeth decided that they would like to move back to Luton, where they were both born and brought up. So with their two youngest children, the Hodge family moved once again, this time to number 99 High Town Road. This space is now occupied by the St. Matthews Infant and Junior Schools. Like many of their previous homes, these premises comprised a retail shop with living accommodation above. This time Elizabeth opened a drapery shop, utilising the skills she had learned as a milliner in her youth. Albert was still working in London and the cost of the daily return train journey, which was 1/7 ¼ (8p), became too great a part of their weekly income. This, together with the trade depression of the time and competition from big stores such as Gamages and Selfridges where sports cycles sold at £5/12/6, or 12 payments of 10/9d, meant the family once again sold up and returned to live in London, this time in Balham.

So ends the early story of Albert Hodge and his family's involvement in the cycle industry. However, a new chapter in Albert's cycle building life was only just beginning and now it was to be with us. After a period of thirty-five years, excluding their brief return in 1930, Albert and Elizabeth Hodge returned to live permanently in Luton. Whilst they had both been born and bred here, they had lived mostly in London since their marriage. Now they moved into a house named "Sunnydale" in Wigmore Lane, which at that time comprised no more than a dozen houses out on the northern edge of the town. It was not long before Albert made contact with the cycling fraternity and decided that he would like to start building his own lightweight cycles again. Luton had become a good centre for cycling activity and the Luton Wheelers, formed in 1900, was well established. So in 1933 Albert started frame building again in a first floor workshop at 19A Francis Street, very near to the Gas Works. He was now 56 years old and very soon became affectionately known as "Pop". The following year Elizabeth found a retail premises at 56A Dumfries Street with a view to opening a drapery shop, but Albert won the day and acquired the shop for his own use whilst Elizabeth found alternative premises in Langley Street. So Albert once again set himself up in full time business in Dumfries Street, in the two storey building on the corner with Windsor Walk where he became The Holly Motor & Cycle Company. The ground floor was stocked with an assortment of cycle spares but Pop's main interest was in the building of frames. The idea of a tidy and attractive display was of little interest to him. Customers had to step over piles of rims, tyres and boxes of spares, but despite the disorder Pop usually had what was wanted and often at a low price, very often too low a price. However, despite his business failings, he did become established in his home town of Luton. In addition to building his own cycles, Pop supplied frames to Charlie Cole at Dunstable for sale under the Cole name. Just along Windsor Walk from the shop was the Luton depot of Wall's Ice Cream

Ltd. and at that time ice cream street trading was carried out by box tricycle. These were serviced by Pop and it was a common sight to see one undergoing repair upended in the road outside the shop. The shop was too small and too cluttered to allow them inside! The problem was usually a broken chain caused by the sheer weight of the fully laden tricycles!

The method of frame building used by Pop had not changed from that used at the turn of the century when he learned his craft. The brazing of all the main tubes was done in a hearth of hot coke which provided soft soaking heat. Additional heat for brazing the joints came from a hand held gas torch, run off the town gas supply, into which air was blown via a foot operated bellows. During this work Pop would usually be singing at the top of his voice. Frame alignment and the brazing of stays, bridges and fittings were done whilst the frame was clamped in a bench vice, the same vice and bench which he used all his working life. To produce a frame with a short wheelbase, Pop would pull the lugs to give a 71 degree head angle, cut short the back stays and reduce the fork rake to one inch. A wheelbase of about 40" was ideal for hill climbs and track racing. By 1936 Pop was agent for Dunlop and Palmer tyres, Cantilever brakes and Tri-Velox gears. With his business increasing, Pop opened a second shop in nearby Wellington Street to allow the Dumfries Street premises to be used solely for frame building. The new shop was at number 57, two doors away from the old Wellington Cinema and now under the Stuart Street dual carriageway. It was in a room above this shop that the Luton Arrow Cycling Club held their inaugural meeting. About the same time, Albert's son Dennis opened a cycle shop in Bury Park Road. Although he stocked Hodge frames, he ran his shop as a completely separate business. Pop also opened a shop in Cauldwell Street, Bedford, but both this and Dennis's shop in Luton did not survive for very many years. In 1938 Pop and his wife moved their home from Wigmore Lane to 26 Rondini Avenue.

The halcyon days of cycling were brought to an end in September 1939 when WW2 was declared and Pop was drafted into the essential war effort, namely munitions work with the Adamant Engineering Company in Dallow Road. Pop was now 62 and it

The Francis Street premises (CH)

was the second time that war had interrupted his career. Both the Wellington Street and Dumfries shops were closed and the remaining stock was moved back to the Francis Street premises, where after his day job Pop would continue to do repairs and build a few new frames. He would often work until midnight, eat his supper and fall asleep in his chair. At the end of the war Pop was 68 but continued working at the Adamant until the age of 80 when he was asked to retire! Following resumption of supplies he moved into yet another workshop at 52A Princess Street. Although the entrance opened onto Princess Street, it was behind Cole's Grocery Shop on the corner with Adelaide Street and had been a dairy before the war. It had a little office in which a few cycle parts were displayed. In the corner was a Dickensian writing desk and on the walls were photographs of racing cyclists. Pop's workshop soon became a haven once again for club cyclists and they would often help Pop build their own frames.

During 1964 Pop's health began to fail and he and Elizabeth moved nearer to their son John's home in Tottenham where they lived quietly until their deaths, only six months apart, in 1966. Albert "Pop" Hodge was 89. So ends his story; he was an ordinary, yet extraordinary, man. He lived through an era that saw the development of the pedal cycle progress from high ordinary to sleek racing bicycle. His contribution has largely been overshadowed by those that followed him, such as Claud Butler.

The Princess Street premises (CH)

However Pop was there in the beginning, innovating and developing new ideas and later being witness to many of his earlier designs used in nearly every modern lightweight cycle. Pop may not have made a fortune from his years of cyclebuilding, but he was rich in the pleasure and satisfaction he gained from his craft. He was generous in the help and advice he gave to both aspiring and seasoned cyclists, and his ability to treat everyone as equals endeared him to all.

I am most grateful to Chris Hewitt, who lives in Harpenden, for allowing me to glean and use much of this story and the photographs from his own book "The Story of A.J.Hodge & His Cycles" which was published in 1991 and records more fully Pop's life in the cycle industry outside of Luton and also the technical achievements of his cycle frames in much greater detail. Copies of this book are still available from the author or from book shops quoting ISBN 0 9511252 1 4.

J. HORTON & CO.
CORN FLOUR & SEED STORES

To the majority of Luton residents nowadays, The Biscot Mill is one of our welcoming restaurants, but the name recalls a windmill which originated in the reign of Elizabeth I and responded to the winds for three and a half centuries. It once crowned the rising ground there and was surrounded by open countryside. Lutonians 'out for a walk' would take Moor Path, an open public footpath which led to the mill following much of the line of the present Biscot Road and then it continued down to Biscot and Limbury. Many millers worked there and William Drewett became the owner of a rebuilt mill in 1855 after it was struck by lightning and destroyed by fire. William was a devoted Quaker and was also in business as a baker in Park Street. His son, also William, continued work at Biscot and in this connection also had a shop in Cheapside for the sale of corn and products from the mill.

Our story begins in 1851 when Jabez Horton was born in the village of Limbury. As a young boy, Jabez worked for William Drewett at that notable landmark, Biscot Mill. He was later transferred to be an assistant at the Cheapside shop and in due course, winning the entire confidence of his employers, became virtually the manager of the retail business. Eventually Jabez took over the Cheapside establishment from Mr. Drewett and later widened its scope, his brother Abner also helping out. Jabez married Elizabeth Shackleton who was three years his junior in 1874. They set up home at number 3 Old Bedford Road and had six children, Annie, Rose, Josiah, Walter, Gertrude and Stanley.

Jabez, Walter and Stanley Horton (JH)

Jabez was an active member of the Wesleyan Methodist Church in Waller Street, Luton, and recalled, as a boy, church services being held in his home. In 1915, in their circuit magazine (price one penny), he says "My father was a farm labourer and received only the small wages given to that class of workers, but he denied himself in order to keep me at school as long as possible. My home influences were always helpful. Both my parents were Christians, and by teaching and example sought to lead their family to follow after the true and good." Jabez engaged in Sunday School teaching, was led to become a local temperance preacher and for fourteen years was Secretary to the Quarterly Meeting.

Their business at 3 Cheapside prospered, sited between the confectioner Denis Robinson and Covington's, the tobacconists. J. Horton & Co. became noted corn, seed and forage merchants and a telephone was installed. You just asked the operator for Luton 23. The family home at 3 Old Bedford Road, which was where the grassed triangle is now, adjacent to Villa Road, was modified so that the front room could also become a shop. There was ample room at the rear for the delivery cart and the stabling of their horse 'Flower', or was it 'Flour'? In Frederick Street, a further building was used as a stores. Jabez took an honourable place in the commerce of the town and

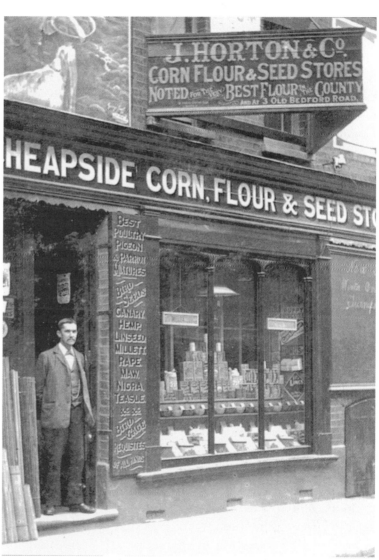

3 Cheapside, c1900, with Abner in the doorway (JH)

for many years shared in municipal work, seeking to advance the best interests of the Borough. For fourteen years he was a Town Councillor and for six years had the honour of being an Alderman. There was often a twinkle in his eye, for he had a lively sense of humour and his witty retorts often brightened the proceedings of the Council Chamber. He was one of the council officials on board the first Luton tram to operate on the opening day in 1908.

The Cheapside shop is still remembered by many. They called it The Cheapside Corn, Flour and Seed Store, noted for the very best Flour in the County. On the outside, next to the window, customers were advised that they sold 'Best poultry, pigeon and parrot mixtures' and a wide choice of bird seeds was listed- 'canary, hemp, linseed, millett, rape, maw, nigra and teasle'. A fixed blackboard was used for current information, such as ' Now selling, Winter Onions and Turnips'. Inside there was a rich, pleasing, country smell, sturdy wooden counters and a wooden floor, sometimes strewn with spilled corn, but always quickly swept up, as was the outside pavement every morning. In addition to the products for which they were highly regarded, flower pots and peasticks were also on sale, indeed they became valued as seedsmen, bulb importers and horticultural sundriesmen. Their own 'Horton's Select Seeds' were packeted, all tested in accordance with the provisions of the Seeds Act of 1920. A wooden lift was used to carry the sacks of corn and flour up to the two upper storage floors. This was manually operated by pulling on long ropes and an internal communication tube existed which necessitated blowing soundly through it to gain attention. Before WW2 the opening hours were 9am to 7pm, but they remained open until 9pm on Saturdays. The busiest period in the shop was over Easter when it was seed potato time. The potatoes were stored at Frederick Street where great care had to be taken if frost was possible overnight. To help enliven the quiet Christmas trade, Jabez placed in his shop window, a clockwork contrivance in a glass case. It portrayed a cat reaching up its paw towards a pheasant but, just before the capture could be made, an old woman opened her mouth and banged down a besom broom. It missed the frightened cat, of course, and so the little comedy was played over and over again. Two live well-fed Persian cats lived in, whose job it was to control the local mouse population.

Jabez had died in 1917, but two sons, Walter and Stanley, had already joined him in the family business and were very capable to continue it. Walter had contributed from the age of 15, but Stanley had earlier trained as an apprentice in the building trade. Walter had married local girl Pemily Nelson, living first in Clarendon Road and later at 17 Alexandra Avenue. Stanley married Norfolk girl Violet Coulson and they lived all their lives at number 4 Havelock Rise. They were both able to celebrate their golden weddings. The two brothers traded as partners in the shop, always wearing white laundered coats, for a further forty years. However, in 1957, J. Horton & Co. closed down. Many customers were surprised, for Stanley was still an agile 70 and Walter did not look 75. Hundreds of people said they were sorry to see them go. "I suppose it will be a bit of a wrench," Walter said, " but we have got to the age when we have begun to feel we should like a rest." Stanley expected to be busy with his work for the Methodist Church and Walter hoped to devote more time to his hobby of photography.

A bent wood measure strengthened with iron banding which had been used in the shop was donated by Stanley to the Luton Museum in Wardown Park. It is stamped 'VR327' and 'Borough of Luton' below a crown, dating from about 1875.

Its capacity was 1 pottle, which equals a quarter of a peck. Stockwood Craft Museum displays a number of items from the old shop. Below the sign for corn merchants Tooley's is the large bank of wooden drawers which came from Horton's. These were used for storage of very many varieties of seeds and the labels are still readable. Also corndressing shears and a scoop, a sack filler and platform and suspension scales were also originally theirs. Believed to have been the oldest corn and seed merchants in Luton, trading for more than eighty years, Horton's time in Luton was over. Number 3 Cheapside still stands and is occupied now by Quicksilver. Stanley's daughter, Janet, is still resident in Luton.

Janet, aged 3, advertising Spratts Dog Food (JH)

SPORTS

I wrote in my first local history book of a man who filled his life with so many interests and enterprises that I named him 'Luton's very own Action Man'. Well, I am confident and without doubt that here we have 'Luton's very own Action Woman'!

It was not easy, one sunny afternoon over an al-fresco lunch in her garden, to note all of Joyce's ventures. To detail all her activities here would consume too many pages, so the next two paragraphs will be just a summary of her many absorbing, intriguing and in some cases unusual pursuits. After Luton High School, Joyce Smith unconventionally studied mechanical engineering at George Kent's and also bought her first second-hand BSA Bantam motor-cycle for £10; played for Luton Rangers, which later amalgamated with Chiltern Ladies' Hockey Club and also played cricket at County level; she joined the WRAF but it was subsequently found that being the only woman Ground Radar Mechanic (qualified in GEE), the only postings involved being billeted on shifts in Nissen huts on hilly outposts, the rest of the teams being men and it was considered that "it wouldn't do" (she was, being the smallest, always the one sent up the dipole for repairs, in all weathers!); so she remustered and duly qualified in Physical Training which in those days included sports ground and equipment maintenance; after four years of many adventures and a tour in the Far East during "the troubles" in Malaya she returned to civvy street; she worked as a photographic assistant in Napier's Research Department until the school year began; in 1956 Joyce filled a gap year at Stopsley Girls' Secondary Modern School teaching PE and Art; missing the buzz of the WRAF, re-entered, took PE further and qualified in Medical Rehabilitation working at specialist RAF stations Chessington, Headley Court and Halton Hospital, meanwhile playing and learning more of all the sports she loved; among many other adventures including mountaineering, climbing, skiing, snow survival and parachuting, she took a very secure train carriage full of sports women through Russian occupied Germany, during the Cold War, to give isolated service women in West Berlin a bit of competition (there's another story of, after an evening out exploring the nightlife of West Berlin, inadvertently going one stop too far on the underground, rising to ground level in the Russian sector and being in civvies with no passes, taking two hours of negotiations to get back into West Berlin!); at the 1962 Biggin Hill Air Show she demonstrated for the first time in this country the Lemoigne Device, a novel, hairy French invention for peeping over a hill at the enemy, in which the driver of a vehicle at speed takes up the slack of a laid out rope, the parachustist running like the clappers is launched up to take photographs, descends, gathers all up and gets quickly away. This has evolved into a much safer sport enjoyed at seaside resorts. Joyce's demo took her to 1000 ft above the airfield for the enjoyment of the spectators, releasing on the last demo and using a prototype that didn't steer, but could candle!

And there's more!; in Germany, during a stint as Recorder at NATO Golf Championships, her car was hit by an Englishman driving at speed on the wrong side of the road. Long stay in Wegberg and then Halton hospitals, then on for rehabilitation where she was back on duty taking the classes she should have been in; on medical discharge, went on crutches to St.Loye's College for the Disabled in Exeter to learn a sedentary trade, shorthand, typing and office procedures for which she is very grateful,

Joyce demonstrating the Lemoigne Device at the 1968 Biggin Hill Air Show (JS)

"so handy", got a secretarial post, went bananas and was then fortunately offered a job at Lillywhite's, the eminent sports group; here she was employed to advise architects on the equipment installation requirements in the design of international and national sports centres and then equipping them through Lillywhite's; in between Joyce raced her Alfa Romeo, changed to a Morgan and enjoyed trialling; and all this before opening her sports shop in Luton. Yet she says "I was not good at anything, but dabbled in it all."

Joyce was born in 1934, daughter of Chippenham man Arthur "Pem" Smith and Bedford girl Dot, who had set up home in Churchill Road, Luton, later moving to Stanford Road. Pem apprenticed at Boosey & Hawkes, made the altar and processional crosses for the new St. Andrew's Church which, from the top of Stockingstone Hill, he and Dot had earlier seen being built in the middle of the country and wondered why. He started South Beds Metal Company at the junction of Villa and Old Bedford Roads, moved to Albert Road and finally, Harvey Smith (Luton) Ltd., at Bilton Road on the Dallow Industrial Estate. He died in 1972 at his home in Lilley.

In 1992, at the age of 58, Joyce (sometimes recognized as Smudge or Smiffy), not enjoying retirement, opened her sports shop, JS Sports, initially in the old joinery at Slip End and then in a shop in Neville Road, Luton, which building had previously been a grocer's. She was determined that it would be a hardware shop for sportsmen and women, not a

JS Sports in Neville Road

the equipment for the new Arlesey F.C. home. For twelve years JS Sports was a successful independent business despite major sports chains opening branches in the area, but in 2003, with the big seven-oh on the horizon, Joyce decided to take well-earned retirement at her Luton home. The shop's respected name remains with the well-known cricket coach, Mohammed Nazir, as the new owner. Joyce said, smiling, 'the shop kept me off the streets, it was great fun, a bit hectic at times to put it mildly and I made many friends.' She is certainly on the streets now in her sporty 1972 Morgan Classic, attending Morgan Owner Club events all over the country. Wonder Woman indeed!

fashion shop selling expensive designer wear for poseurs. She wanted it to be the sort of shop where anyone could come in and get good advice on the correct size and standard of cricket bat, hockey stick, ball or protective gear. Joyce said 'I supply for sportsmen and women to play in.' Sports clubs, schools and councils throughout Britain and overseas (even Argentina just after the war) became customers and without the internet, for she could never master computers. Equipment and clothing for virtually every sport was stocked, soccer, rugby, cricket, hockey, lacrosse, martial arts, netball as well as school PE uniforms. All this was in stock, only big equipment going direct from the factories. Examples were goals, sight screens and cricket nets to Great Barford; sets of rugby posts to the new location for Luton Rugby Club and

Joyce on her retirement day   (JS)

JOHNSONS CAFE

I like a nice cup of tea in the morning and a nice cup of tea with my tea and when it's time for bed there's a lot to be said for a nice cup of tea…..tra la! I wonder if you can put the music to those words of long ago. It must surely be the theme song of the Johnson family who poured tea for the people of Luton for 38 years.

William Edward Johnson, Bill to everyone, was at the age of 14, believed to be the youngest qualified auctioneer in Middlesborough where he was born in 1878. He married Yorkshire girl Gertrude Longden and together they had six children. In 1917 Gertrude, her five children and Gertrude's sisters Alma, Anice and Evelyn travelled south to Luton where they gained work in local factories engaged in supporting the war effort. Bill was serving in the Durham Light Infantry. The sixth son Bob was born in Luton in 1925. Bill and his family lived at no.13a Holly Walk and he commenced his Luton businesses with an antique furniture and bric-a-brac shop at no.6 Church Street. He also held auctions of household furniture and effects at The Franklin Hotel in George Street. One of his expiration-of- lease auctions contained 465 miscellancous lots including wool mattresses, feather beds and bolsters, straw palliasses, a large oilograph, a mangle, a copper urn and a bath geyser (burst!). This shop was successful until the open market on Park Square was ended which reduced his customers to the point of bankruptcy and closure. He then spent a number of years as a conductor with the local bus company.

The tea brewing began in 1929 when Gertrude opened their first tea shop on the corner of Adelaide Street and Hastings Street but Bill stayed with the buses for a short time. Good tea and pies and buns were served here until 1933 when, wanting a larger shop and more customers, they took over 23 Park Street. The more central premises next to house furnishers Charles Farmbrough and on the corner with Church Street extended through to no.2 Church Street. A very old building with a well in the cellar, which was not discovered until the day an armchair fell into it. The bottom of the

Bill Johnson (DJ)

The Park Street café (DJ)

counter and said "Where you've been taking pennies, you'll soon be taking pounds!" Bill was an accomplished piano player and often gave a tune inside the café. Sometimes the police had to ask him to stop playing as the crowds outside listening to him were forming an obstruction on the pavement. During WW2 anyone in uniform who bought a cup of tea was always given a second cup free of charge. William and Gertrude moved their home around the town many times, Cowper Street, Cromwell Road, Barton Road, Carlton Crescent, to the point that when the removal company were telephoned they would gasp "Oh no, not that big piano again!"

A paragraph here about the other Johnsons Café! The Adelaide Street shop had been taken over in 1933 by Bill's son John when his parents moved

well could not be seen. This café became well known and frequented by many Lutonians not only for the 'nice cup of tea' which cost one old penny, but also for the favourite meal which was pie, chips and peas. Quite often queues would form outside. With this success a visit by a gypsy to the earlier shop was recalled, for she had looked at them squarely over the

At Park Street are (l to r) Elsie Johnson, Bertha, Bob Johnson, Gertrude Johnson, Hetty, Florrie and Lil White (DJ)

to Park Street. John was known to all as Jack and his wife Marjorie (nee Tompkins), was known to all as Madge. She was a Dunstable girl and with Jack they lived in Periwinkle Lane in Dunstable for many years Jack was once a promising footballer until an injury brought this to a halt, when he joined the Eastern National Omnibus Company and became their youngest driver. Jack's son John, who now lives in Hampshire, recalls that early morning bread-rolls were purchased from Mc.Hattie's bakery in Stuart Street, cakes from Timbury's in Princess Street and steak and kidney and pork pies and sausage rolls from G.A.Wallers in Dunstable Road. Morning opening at 6am created a great deal of passing trade from the Walls Ice Cream depot in Windsor Walk, from Hubbards felt mill in Regent Street and many hat factories nearby. A good reputation was established and the café slogan was "Jacks for snacks and tea you can drink". These premises had previously been a bakery and John remembers that there were ovens and a well in the cellar beneath the café, a stable across the covered yard with a manger, a well and a wooden double-seated toilet which was smooth with wear. This business was sold when Jack died, aged 52.

At the end of hostilities Bill's sons Bob and Harry joined their father in the Park Street cafe, but Harry died shortly after aged only 47 and Bill died in 1950. Both Bob and Harry played drums in local bands, Harry with The Victoria Players and Bob with The Ken Horwood Band. Lil White who was originally employed on a temporary basis stayed as cook at Park Street and Castle Street for 33 years.

The Castle Street café (DJ)

Ann, Rose, Bertha, and Florrie worked on a rota as washers-up. Bob was at the counter and his wife Dorothy was always there wherever needed. In 1948 Bob had married Dorothy Cook at St. Mary's Church in Luton, they had met whilst taking dancing lessons at Mrs. Brown's dancing school in Rothesay Road. Dorothy had been evacuated from her London school, the North Western Polytechnic, sharing premises during the war with the Luton High School for Girls. She remembers well that the High School girls would not speak to them! The compulsory purchase of properties 23 to 31 Park Street in 1956 to enable extensions to the Luton & South Bedfordshire College of Further Education, now the University of Luton, forced the Johnsons to re-locate at 15 Castle Street and here Bob and Dorothy became renowned for providing unrivalled food of good value for the working people of Luton. It was a working man's café with a friendly atmosphere and became virtually a local institution. A juke box had been installed there during the war which attracted many American servicemen. It was retained in the family café and daughter June recalls as a child being given 3d bits by customers for singing along with it. The regulars included workers from the Whitbread Brewery, Vauxhall Motors, the bus depot and local shops and offices.

Once again the property which Bob had bought became the subject of a compulsory purchase when the Stuart Street inner-ring road was built and parts of Castle Street were demolished. The

Dorothy and Bob Johnson (DJ)

position of the café is now under Flowers Way. So Bob retired from the catering trade in 1971, going on to work as a pensions visitor for Whitbread for ten years and later with Shaw & Kilburn. He finally retired in 1990. He and Dorothy had two daughters and one son and seven grandchildren and they celebrated their golden wedding in June 1998 but sadly Bob died only eight months later. Dorothy still lives in Luton.

Had it not been for the compulsory purchasing of both of their well-remembered eating places, is it possible that the Johnson family would still be feeding us?…but then that's another cup of tea!

ASH KAY

Long before the days of the European Union, it was Milan which gave the law to all European matters, including dress. A corruption of Milaner became the name given to those who designed and decorated the fashionable headware of the time, the milliner.

Harry Ashley Kay (PK)

As WW2 came to an end Harry Ashley Kay and his wife Kitty were living in the Greater London district of Totteridge. Harry was a milliner and he travelled each day to John Street in the city, where he was a junior partner in a prosperous concern producing ladies hats. However, this came to an abrupt end one Monday morning when it was realised that the senior partner was missing, as also were the company records. He had left for South Africa with the entire bank balance of cash, which had been withdrawn on the previous Friday afternoon.

With decisions to be made rather quickly, Harry decided to bring his abilities to the national home of the hat manufacturing industry, Luton. So in 1949 Harry Kay (Millinery) Ltd. was born at the rear of a house at 69 North Street. Kitty took on the task of sales, travelling in an aged van which had been borrowed. On wet days it allowed the rain in through what they called "the pneumonia hole". However within a year they had become successfully established, having brought with them to Luton all their old customers from the defunct company in London. Their achievement necessitated a move in 1957 to 17 Williamson Street, premises previously occupied by Mr Mendel in a similar business. More staff were employed, but about five years later yet another move had to be made when Williamson Street was totally lost to the Arndale Centre compulsory purchases. They were the first to move into a new building at 10 Old Bedford Road, rebuilt following a destructive fire. Here commerce really took off, helped by a contract with the international company C & A. Staff had increased to 84 and now included Kitty and Harry's son Peter and his wife Norma. Previously Peter had been an engineer designing turbine blades for Rolls Royce and Norma was a fashion artist. It was about this time that major hat factories in Luton were beginning to close, so the two generations of the Kay family had to decide what to do. Peter and Norma researched the rag trade, and in 1964 the decision was taken to try producing suede skirts. They freely admit to having had no idea at the time of how to do this, but were determined to stay in business and initially purchased second-hand machines for a trial period. Once again the venture was a big success, following with leather coats for both ladies and men, and flying jackets and motorcycle wear were also a possibility.

Sales agreements were forged with big outlets C & A and Burtons. The swinging sixties created a new demand. Mini-skirts were the young fashion and so the company produced one of its most popular ranges, the suede or leather mini-skirt. In addition 1,800 jackets were now being made each month for Burtons.

The final move of premises to the upstairs floor of an old hat factory next to Coupees Path in Midland Road was made in 1972. It was at this time that their own hat manufacturing was ended. This building had previously been used by Swiss straw-hat manufacturers Paul Walser & Co. In the late 1980s, as winters became less cold and the demand for sheepskin coats fell off, the next move was into an extensive cushion making facility, once again in suede and leather. When purchase tax was replaced by V.A.T., selling direct to the public became more practical, so as AshKay, Peter decided to try his hand at this new venture, although they were still producing 450 jackets a week on a two year contract with Burtons. Over the years AshKay made leather clothing for many rock and pop celebrities. Internationally

Peter Kay in the Midland Road factory (PK)

acclaimed performers would land their private jet at Luton Airport and taxi to Midland Road to place orders for leather jackets for their forthcoming world tours. Quite often 200 items would be ordered for their entire entourage, the jackets being used as a recognizable pass into their security controlled areas. It was at this time that imported clothing of a lesser quality from Hong Kong, Korea, India, Pakistan and China began to kill the business. There was plenty of work but very little profit to be made. As this era came to an end, Peter said "We still have lots of customers who have been with us for years. We still get people saying 'I bought this coat from you 28 years ago and I'm still wearing it. Can I have a new lining?'" However, Peter says that he has very much enjoyed the years of dealing directly with the public. It has been great fun and he loves Lutonians.

In 2002 AshKay Ltd., one of Luton's most popular factory shops, came to the end of its lease and closed after more than 30 years and more than 50 years of the family business. Harry died in 1984, aged 75, and Kitty died seven years later. However, Peter Kay now has yet another new venture. Kay Aviation Seating in Windsor Walk is producing leather seating for the smaller budget airlines.

Peter Kay in his new role, cutting material for Virgin first-class airline seats

Leather seats are economical, being easily cleaned and lasting possibly 10 years. Working with him will be long-serving employee Wendy Read who lives in the local village of Cockernhoe. She joined AshKay in 1968 when she was 16 and is still with the firm. Peter and Norma live in Barnet and they have three grown-up children. Norma has retired but Peter, whose hobby is restoring classic Jaguar cars, can still be found at 8.30 am every morning, busy in his new Luton venture.

Lacey's
"The House that Value Built."

Men are traditionally conservative in their dress, certainly more so a century ago than they are today. The gentlemen's outfitter in that time has catered from bowler and pin-stripes and cloth cap and muffler to shirt and braces and plus-fours and pullover. The clothier, tailor, outfitter and juvenile specialist in this story is one that boys and men of Luton will recollect, for Lacey's were with us through three generations of their family.

William George Lacey, one of a family of six children, was a native of Luton but his father William James was born in 1833 in Hemel Hempstead and lived only until he was 37. William George, who was born in 1858, had very little schooling, for he started work in the

men's department at the age of 11 with Mr. George Strange, who in those days occupied premises where the Corn Exchange was built. He subsequently became a partner with Mr. Strange's son Harry. They were partners for some years at Strange's new shop at 38 Wellington Street. William George had by now married Sarah Connolly and they had two children whilst living at Lynwood which was 45 Brook Street, where the garden backed onto the Moor. Alexander was born in 1885 and Millie in 1891. The business partnership was successful for many years but eventually "it didn't work with pleasure", noted Millie. In 1909 William George opened his own small shop, together with his 24 year old son Alexander, at 14 Wellington Street, previously occupied by The General Hardware Company. Alexander's father had sent him straight from school to gain experience at outfitters Tearney & Co. in Maidstone. He was there a few years

William, Alexander and Derrick Lacey (ML)

before moving to their Stratford branch. After that, together with a Mr. Harry Parsons, he ran a shop that his father had in St. Albans. When this closed he joined his father in Luton and Lacey & Son was born. One year later Alexander married Lillia Clay and they lived in Leagrave Road. In his spare time, and with Mr. Blundell and Mr. Facer, Alexander helped to build a "Flying Flea" aeroplane which he later hoped to learn to fly. Alexander owned one of the very few Chrysler cars in the area and some years later the engine from this vehicle was used as the winch at the London Gliding Club at the foot of Dunstable Downs.

With assistants Harry Parsons, Mr S. Mc.George and Mr A. Hill, father of Leslie Hill who was once landlord of The Granville public house in Cheapside,

business in bustling Wellington Street prospered and extensions were soon necessary. Old stables at the rear of the premises were converted to form part of the boy's department, which was a few steps up from the main floor and will be remembered by many Luton Modern and Grammar School pupils who were taken there when their parents bought the school uniform. The first floor above the shop became part of the new men's clothing department which could be accessed via a spiral staircase. At this time navy suits, made to measure, cost 25/- (£1.25), tweed overcoats sold for 21/- (£1.05p), a shirt could be bought for 1/11 (10p), socks for 6 1/2d (3p) a pair and hats were 2/6 (12 1/2p) each. In 1910 they advertised that they had clothes for all seasons, fancy vests and straw hats for Spring, tennis shorts and boys' washing

Queues at the Lacey's sale of 1921 (ML)

blouses for Summer, in the Autumn there were felt hats and leggings and hosiery and heavy suitings for Winter. Few men, however, could afford to take time off work to buy a suit of clothes, so Lacey's senior assistant spent much of his time visiting customers at their place of work to measure them for suits. One of their best customers was a Mr Denby who worked

Queues at the Lacey's sale of 1921 (ML)

at Biscot Mill, when it was a working mill and still set among the surrounding cornfields. In 1921, during the great slump, one of the greatest ever sales in Luton took place. Money was short and the company found themselves with large stocks of men's suits and overcoats on the shelves. The decision was taken to sell out stocks quickly and the wholesale slashing of prices resulted in queues gathering outside the shop for four days, past S.Hilton & Sons boot stores and Mr. Prosser's Cox's Pharmacy, around the corner into Peel Street. A policeman and an army sergeant were at the door to control the crowds. All stock was cleared and over £4000 taken in the four days, a very large sum at that time.

When William George Lacey died in 1925, his wife having predeceased him by five years, Alexander took control of the business. William George had been a keen Liberal all his life. In his early years he attended the Union Chapel but later worshipped at the Parish Church. Representatives of the wholesale clothing trade attended his funeral at the General Cemetery which was conducted by Rev. Jaquet. Alexander and his wife Lillia had five children. The two daughters were Sheila and Daphne and the sons were Alexander jnr, Derrick and Raymond, who all attended Bedford School. Alexander jnr, who was always known as Buzz, died in 1941 at the age of 20. As a Flight Lieutenant in the Royal Air Force he was killed during a training flight over fields near Chinnor. The Bishop of Dorchester dedicated a window to his memory in Chinnor Church. Known as "the Airmen's Window" it is believed to be the first time that aeroplanes have appeared in a stained glass window.

Derrick and Raymond followed their

Other staff who may be remembered were Janet and Raymond Standing, Leslie McDonald, Mrs Cook and Mr Fisher.

Alexander Lacey died, aged 72, in December 1957. He had been a Freemason, a member of both local Chambers of Commerce and Trade, the Luton Town Bowling Club, the Liberal Club and the Lansdowne Club. Following his father's death, Derrick and his wife lived at the family home in Lansdowne Road and Monica lives there to this day, for Derrick died in 1971 at the age of only 50 years. Monica has three sons and six grandchildren. Derrick had been a Rotarian, a Freemason, a member of South Beds Golf Club and also Bletchley Sailing Club. He was also a founder member of the Luton Round Table in 1948. Raymond, who had served in a commissioned rank in the Royal Corps of Signals during WW2, was in peacetime a member of the South Beds Golf Club. Following Derrick's death it was decided that the Lacey family business should come to an end. For 63 years Lacey's were at the forefront of skilled men's and boys' outfitting in Luton and are assured of certain recollection by many Lutonians. Number 14 Wellington Street is now Alan Bartram's travel agency.

father into the family business and became partners just after WW2. Raymond married Marie Beasley and lived at 19 Rosslyn Crescent, and Derrick married Monica Tofield and they set up home at 30 Avenue Grimaldi. The family held their staff in great respect, many staying for a considerable number of years. Mr Harold Francis was the longest serving with over fifty years, through three generations of the Lacey family.

LEE'S Cooked Meat

In 1825 the French gastronome Anthelme Brillat-Savarin wrote in his compendium on the art of dining, "One can become a cook, but one is born a roaster of meat". This certainly describes the three generations of the Lee family who roasted meat for the people of Luton for 82 years.

St. Neots' Master Butcher Samuel William Lee married his Welsh girlfriend Caroline Ledsham and together they lived in Wrexham. Three of their children, Percy, Ernest and Cecily were born there before they moved to Luton, where Harold was born in John Street. Many moves were made within Luton during the next few years. Samuel opened his first cooked meat premises at 19 Adelaide Street and his brother Walter opened up at 82 Park Street, but was successful there for only a very short time. Next Sam moved to 27 Hitchin Road on the corner with Duke Street (currently the collector's shop Jenny's Junk) and then again a short move to 10 High Town Road (now the Southern Fried Chicken shop, SFC Express). For some years both traded successfully in this shopping area, but the High Town Road shop was the more permanent, remaining for another 40 years until closure in 1946. During this time both Percy and Harold worked here with their father. The original entrepreneur Samuel died in 1947, only a year after closure, and his wife Caroline, who had worked with him many years at the High Town shop, died in 1954.

The third son, Ernest William, who had worked as an upholsterer in the motor trade with both Rover in Coventry and locally with Vauxhall, married Scarborough girl Lily Crossland in 1927, and three years later he also joined the

Caroline and Samuel Lee   (JL)

10 High Town Road in 1914

Newton Abbot and Bovingdon, he returned to the Wellington Street shop with a greater knowledge and a determination to develop the business further. He also married a Luton girl, Freda Allen, from Lea Road, at St. Mary's Church in 1958. Cecily retired in 1946, Harold joining them at the same time and staying for a further twelve years. Margaret also joined the business at about this time. One non-family member of staff, Roy Foster, was employed straight from school for a further 20 years. John's wife Freda joined the family firm in 1971 and served in the shop for 10 years.

Although there were local competitors such as Durrant's, Waller's, Saxby's and Jones, John and his father were very successful and were proud to state in the shop that they did not use any preservatives in any of their produce, which was all cooked in the oven on the premises and in the 50 gallon stainless-steel boilers. Joints of beef and pork were purchased from Luton wholesalers Swifts and Borthwicks, bacon came from the Herts & Beds Bacon Co. in Hitchin and the Dunmow Bacon Co., and smoked ham from Oakley Bros. Sales could include three hot joints and three whole

family in their chosen trade. Together with his sister Cecily, he opened up in the cooked meat business at 72 Wellington Street where they used a coke-fired oven which was later converted to gas. Wellington Street was one of Luton's main shopping areas at this time and number 72 was part of this before it was cut into two by the inner ring road. Ernest and Lily lived for a short time above the shop, but later moved to 22 Clarendon Road and then to 130A Old Bedford Road. A son, John Michael, was born in the Hitchin Road Nursing Home in 1929 and a daughter Margaret in 1931. After the learning years at Old Bedford Road School, John joined the family team in 1943 at the age of 14, but enlisted in the army at the age of 18. After three years in charge of catering depots at

hams a day, Scotch eggs, steak and kidney and pork pies, sausage rolls, pasties and hundred of faggots, totalling three thousand pastries a week. Northern delicacies were succulent boiled pigs' tails and trotters; black puddings prepared with blood collected direct from the slaughter house; pease pudding in which peas were boiled with pork and beef; faggots, sometimes called "poor man's goose", comprising beef, bread, onion and seasoning; chitterlings, being the pig's smaller intestines prepared for frying or served cold; tripe, which is beef intestines; and pork brawn, in which lean beef is boiled with pig's heads and tongues after removal of the brain and then pressed into a mould. The brains were not sold but could be purchased from butchers, and then cooked, diced and served with a little butter on toast. In 1943 ham sold at 6 pence (2.5p) a quarter pound; pork pies were tuppence ha'penny (approx. 1p); faggots were a ha'penny each and pease pudding was ha'penny a scoop. Children would spend a ha'penny buying a scoop of pease pudding before going to the Wellington Cinema almost opposite, and the story goes that, if they did not like the film, they would throw it at the screen!

In 1981 the tripe and onion brigade were struck a bitter blow when John decided that twelve-hour days starting at 5.30 a.m. were making him, even at the age of 52, too tired. This, together with new E.U. regulations, was making trade difficult, although their cooking was sound and there had never been a complaint against any product. Customers were regarded as friends, one 90 year old walking from Kingsway once a week

John, Margaret and Ernest Lee at the Wellington Street shop in 1981   (JL)

for his pease pudding. So, after 82 years, this old family business closed at the top and 88 year old Ernest was still working and dealing with the accounts until closure on July 11th 1981. He died four years later. No 72 Wellington Street is now the Luton Tandoori Indian Take-Away.

A new life in retirement opened up for John Lee. After two less demanding jobs he spent five enjoyable and busy years in the transport section at Dunstable Police Station. Now final retirement in Stopsley enables him and Freda to enjoy the two grandchildren born to their daughter Jacqueline, and for John to continue his life-long hobby of cycle racing. Not just cycling....cycle racing! A member of the Icknield Racing Club since 1951, and now a life member, he produces times faster than many younger men. He now races at the Manchester Velodrome but in 2002 out on the A1 he achieved the national age record of 22 minutes 50 seconds for 10 miles ...at the age of 72!

John Lee racing his Poyzer Lo-Pro cycle in 1998 (JL)

Perhaps pigs' trotters and faggots offer more than we realise, they obviously create brawn!

We do not use preservatives
Our Daily Cookings & Quick Sales are a guarantee of the freshness of our cooked meats and small goods at all times.

LILLYWHITE (TIMBER) LTD

As a young boy George Cecil Lillywhite had an unhappy childhood, having had a broken arm inaccurately reset which for the rest of his life gave him the inability to lift it correctly; and also being badly treated by his elder brothers who continually subdued him, telling him that he would never amount to anything! This arrogant behaviour bred in him a determination to prove them wrong and this he certainly did in our home town for more than 30 years.

He was born in 1904 at Hurstpierpoint in Sussex, where his father was a butler to a family who sometimes entertained royalty. His first job was with Farquarharsons, leading timber importers and merchants in the East End of London, successfully becoming their chief sales representative. He met Barbara Olive Seaward, one of a family of thirteen children who was born and lived in Tottenham, at The St.Ignatius Tennis Club in London and married in 1935.

They came to Luton in 1940. Barbara's brother G. F. Seaward, who became an Alderman and Luton's mayor in 1946, was already here with his brother Frank and formed the building company Seaward Bros. Another brother Reg, also a builder, and his sister Alice were also in Luton. Barbara and George lived in Blundell Road in a house with a large field to the rear on which they kept chickens, rabbits and geese. It was this field, rented from Seaward Bros, which continued George in the trade for which we remember him locally. He had applied for and gained a permit which allowed him to store and sell wood from this field, initially to his neighbours. During WW2 he was able to supply timber for various projects, including thousands of rungs for the ladders used in the Mulberry Harbour epic. After the war, land was acquired on the corner of Leagrave Road and Waller Avenue, where, in addition to timber sales to the public, a sawing and planing mill was established to carry out work for other merchants and commercial firms such as Electrolux, Hayward-Tyler and Skefko. In addition to the woods we all know, unusual types were also available, such as Agba, Peroba, Makore, Iroko and Avodire. These premises were parallel to the busy railway line along which George wanted to place advertising hoardings,

George Lillywhite (JPa)

96

but permission to do so was not granted. He was not to be beaten, however, and he overcame this problem by having the Lillywhite name spelt out in glass bricks within the brick building facing the track, the lighting from within displaying the name to everyone on the trains that passed. In 1953, after 14 years of control, timber was freed from license. George and his staff celebrated the end of control at the Leagrave Road sawmills by making a big bonfire of the various forms and documents which for so long had been their unwelcome companions.

A Luton head office was opened in Castle Street in 1956, with further storage and production areas being set up in Chiltern Green railway sidings and Houghton Regis. The company had a depot in Stanton Road, Luton and premises were also bought in Capron Road, Dunstable, before Lillywhite's moved to the Skimpot Industrial Estate in 1965 where a new mill was built. Staff in charge at this time were Fred Seabrook at Leagrave Road, Gerry Mann at Stanton Road and Reg Oakins and Alfred Trulock at Houghton Regis. George valued his staff, arranging annual outings and firework parties for all. Then, saying "I've always dealt in dead wood, now I'm going into live wood", in 1963 George Lillywhite opened one of the first garden centres in the district in Grange Avenue and his container roses became very popular. The family had moved into 'the big house' The Grange in Grange Avenue, in 1950.

The Dunstable Road timber yard. (CL)

Lillywhite's float in George Street during the Coronation celebration parade in 1953   (CL)

In 1971 both the Skimpot and Leagrave Road companies were sold to W. H. Newson of Pimlico, although they retained the respected name of Lillywhite. This was later relinquished to the Sabah Group and later again became Harcros. When the Houghton Regis, Douglas Road and Stanton Road sites were sold, the two Lillywhite companies that remained were Lillywhite (Leagrave) Ltd. at Leagrave Road and Lillywhite (Dunstable) Ltd. at the Skimpot Depot. Frank Estall oversaw Leagrave and Stanton Roads and Alfred Trulock was the Group Accounts Controller. George retired from his landscaping company in 1976 when it was taken over by Hank Hooft, his contracts manager. George was well known for his charitable work for the church, youth clubs and The Variety Club of Great Britain. He was also a keen Luton Town Football Club supporter for many years and his firm's amusing advertisements, in which the art work was all his own, were a regular feature of match programmes in the days when the Hatters were also nicknamed the Lilywhites. He had an interest in pencil drawing, with a special ability with animal heads and cathedrals. He was also a philatelist, his main hobby in retirement. In 1950 he was a founder member of the Limbury Boys Club. He

Note the players in this Luton Town FC programme (RW)

was also President of the Luton Corinthians Cricket Club, for whom he gave the Lillywhite Batting Cup.

Mrs. Lillywhite died in 1982 and her husband lived on his own for six years, before going to live with his son Clive near St. Neots. George Lillywhite died aged 86 in December 1990 at Hinchingbrooke Hospital, Huntingdon after a long illness, and the funeral service at Eaton Socon was conducted by the Rev. Basil Jones, former vicar of St. Lukes, Leagrave. The surviving family is Clive, a graphic designer in St. Neots; Marian, a professor of Fine Arts at the University of Missouri and Judy who is still in our area, living in Houghton Regis.

H. H. MOWER
PARK SQUARE
LUTON

Today we would call them DIY stores, but a century ago when our subject opened his shop in Luton he was an ironmonger, a tool merchant, a locksmith, a cutler and more. He was expected to be knowledgeable on all aspects of paints and plumbing, of locks and carpentry.

Herbert Harold Mower was born in Bridgewater in 1882. He met and married Londoner Florence Andrews who was a year younger than he. Florence's parents moved to Luton when her father became manager of Henry Brown's timber yard, so

Florence and Herbert came to Luton at the end of WW1 and were married at the Wellington Street Baptist Church. Herbert worked at first for Jennings & Gates, the ironmongers in George Street, but in his 21st year became a local businessman with his own shop at 7 Park Street, that part which was usually known as Park Square. It stood where the paved area is now in front of Maplin Electronics. Herbert and Florence lived in the two rooms above the shop and whilst they lived there Harold was born. He was later to become the milliner H.S.Mower in Peel Street and Bute Street. The family moved home to 63 Naseby Road and later to 10 Belmont Road, having their three daughters and their second son Thomas who was born in 1919. When he was six

Herbert and Tom Mower   (TM)

years old Thomas contracted diphtheria which meant a six-week stay in the Spittalsea Isolation Hospital for Infectious Diseases. He fully recovered, the hospital being an ideal site 500 feet above sea level, where London Luton Airport is now. In 1933, when Tom was only 13, his mother died aged only 49. Whilst his elder brother was sent to Dunstable Grammar School, Tom attended Dunstable Road and Beech Hill Schools in Luton. Tom did not work for his father at the end of schooldays but took a number of jobs locally, including working with an accountant for 8/6 (42p) a week. This enabled him to approach his father for a sensible wage and he joined him at the age of 15 for a weekly wage of 16/- (80p). Although Tom was to work with his father for 35 years and always on more than 50-hour weeks, their partnership was unfortunately discordant. In 1954 Tom married Betty Rayment, a

nursing sister at the Alexandra Orthopaedic Hospital at Stockwood Park in Luton and they had two children and later two grandchildren.

The shop provided cutlery, engineering tools, ironmongery, scissors, shears, lawnmowers, key cutting and grinding and there was a time when 50 dozen open razors were kept in stock. When the shop opened, the cattle market stretched from Park Square to the Luton Hoo gates and Herbert could remember hearing the Luton Red Cross Band play in the Square and also recalled the auctions held there which he used to call 'the rubbish heaps'.

7 Park Street, c1930s (TM)

In the 1930s Mowers could supply a Yale key for 9d. (4p) and there was a Yale cutting machine for this, but mortice keys were originally made by hand. Nails were 6d. (2p) per lb. Screws could be bought by the dozen, or less, and chain was measured along the brass yardstick set in the counter. Tom recalls cutting two keys for the doors of Wrest House in Silsoe without having the samples to match. The beautiful locks which were brought to the shop measured 12"x 8" and were skilfully made in brass, every component being removable and intricately fitting together. The two hand-made keys took six hours work and cost £3 each. Another key hand-made for the lock of a local church transpired to be in the form of the holy cross when completed. In the early days Tom used to run across the road to Gibbons, the furniture and clothing shop, to get cups of tea for his father. They also served, for 3/6 (17p), afternoon teas in their tea room where there was often an orchestra playing. Behind the counter in the shop there were over 300 drawers, each containing stock and they knew what was in each of them! Some of these drawers are still in use in a mechanic's workshop in Cambridge. Two slogan cards were on view to customers and they read "The man who loans tools is 'out'", and "All the world is queer, save thee and me, and even thee's a little queer!" Mowers were agents for Robbialac paints which were ordered by their initials, ie. RG for Robbialac Glossy and RU for the Undercoat, followed by a number which denoted a specific colour.

Tom chuckles when he thinks of the customer who asked for one of their products and Tom, confirming this, said RU 17? The young man looked surprised and said "No…do you have to be?"

The Aladdin's cave that was Mower's bustling shop, and which always overflowed its displays onto the pavement, closed when the premises were taken over by compulsory purchase by Luton Council for the building of the Arndale Shopping Centre. There was a closing-down sale in December 1970. Later a one-day sale offered everything at half-price, and then the queue of prospective customers stretched right down to Blundell's furniture shop, with some retailers complaining that customers could not get into their premises. When this row of shops was demolished, the last wall to fall was one within the Mower's building and which was known to be 450 years old. Also behind the shop, before demolition, there was an inhabited cottage with a beautiful dahlia garden which had access from Smiths Lane.

Herbert Mower, who lived at 113 Wardown Crescent, was a lifelong teetotaller, had been a member of the Luton Choral Society, of the Luton Amateur Operatic Society and also the Luton Cricket Club. He had been keen on swimming and football and was a keen supporter of Luton Town Football Club. In May 1943 he was presented with a 'smoker's companion' to commemorate his 21 years as President of the Luton Angling Club. Often late on Saturday evenings, anglers would bring their catch

Along Park Street, Mower's is the shop with the long narrow sunblind

into the shop to be weighed. The weekly report of angling news for the 'Luton News' was prepared at the shop every Monday morning. Herbert died in 1972, aged 90. With the passing of the shop Tom commenced his second career as an administrative assistant at the Luton College of Higher Education (now the University), where he spent the next thirteen years before retirement. Sadly Tom's wife died in March 2003, but Tom is kept busy with church work and playing the organ in several local churches. Happily he is still recognized by many satisfied customers from the days of H.H.Mower, the "DIY" shop which served the people of Luton for 67 years.

H. NEALE & SON

Some of the most nourishing foods we eat are those which nature has provided and milk is almost unique among animal foods in that it contains all three nutrients; proteins, carbohydrates and fats. You will realise that this story concerns one local family who spent their working lives delivering this most important part of our diet.

In the early nineteenth century, the Neale family were farm workers living in and around the villages in the west of Bedfordshire between Dunstable and Woburn. John Neale, who was born in 1831, was described in the 1881 census as a 'baker journeyman'. He married Elizabeth Smith from the village of Eversholt and their son Henry was born in Hockliffe in 1861. Eventually Henry also married into a branch of the Smith family, Helen being the daughter of Jonathan Smith, a master blacksmith. Henry and Helen were married at Chalgrave parish church in 1887 and set up home in Eggington where, with a fellow villager, Henry was a local carter and haulier.

By 1891, Henry and his family had moved to Luton, where they made their home at 13 Burr Street,

which is where their dairy business would be established and where four generations of the Neale family would come to call home. Helen and Henry had five children, their second son Charles (Charlie) eventually joining his father in the family concern. Their youngest daughter Millicent was remembered as being the first woman to be married at the Central Mission in Midland Road. Another son, Theodore, became a director of the hat company Currant & Creak. The family home and dairy premises at one time comprised both numbers 13 and 15 Burr Street, with large double gates between the houses which led to a covered yard where the milk-cart was stored and beyond that to a small open cobbled yard extending towards Gillam Street. On the left of the back yard was a high wall, behind which was Tommy Plowman's garage situated at the

Louisa and Charles Neale (BN)

corner of Burr Street and Hitchin Road, while on the right was a small stable block with an upper storey with hutches where rabbits were bred. Ahead lay a large brick dairy where Helen (and later her daughter-in-law) would wash and clean the large upright milk churns and pails used in the milk business. There was also an outside privy and other out-houses. Inside the house at number 13, the front parlour was used as the milk shop, which has been described as being 'snow white', with a big china swan in the bay window. There were wooden cupboards and a large wooden counter on the linoleum covered floor, and the shop was lit by gas mantles. Helen served in the shop and is remembered as having her hair drawn back, looking very severe, filling the jug with milk and handing it back without a word or a smile. It was possibly not realised that, for most of her life, Helen had been totally blind.

The family lived at the rear of the house, where there was a back parlour and a large stone-flagged kitchen-cum-scullery leading to the yard and dairy.

Henry, known to most as Harry, was called 'the midnight milkman' because he used to deliver the milk to his customers late in the day, often travelling around preaching the Word both in Luton and in surrounding villages. He was an enthusiastic lay-preacher on the Methodist circuit. Before he could deliver the milk, it had to be collected from a rail depot in Midland Road, from where the horses could easily find their own way home at the end of the working day, quite often at speed. Henry used a three-wheeled, polished brass cart which held the churn in the middle and had pails and scoops hanging on the side. At the time he was remembered, a half-pint of milk cost a ha'penny and skimmed milk cost three ha'pence a quart. Harry would carry the milk on a yoke across his shoulders or customers would take their own jugs out to his cart, or go round to the shop to be served.

Harry died in 1931 and his son Charlie continued the family business. Charles had married Louisa Odell at St. Matthews's Church in 1913; she was a

On the extreme left is 13-15 Burr Street (SSm)

local High Town girl coming from a family living in North Street. The dairy business continued to prosper under Charlie's direction and throughout WW2. From the late 1920s, Charlie was assisted by his elder son Arthur (known to everyone as 'Son'), who extended the business beyond the High Town area when he purchased a motor van and so became the third generation dairyman. Son was called up to serve in the Royal Air Force during the war and, although Charlie continued the business on his own, it became clear that it would be too much for one man. At the end of the war, Son was demobilized and after helping his father for about a year, he joined the workforce of Vauxhall Motors in 1946. He moved away from Burr Street the following year to a new family home in Taunton Avenue with his wife and their young son Barry. In 1941 Arthur had married Barbara Brown who was related to another old Luton retailing family, the Harmans.

By 1950, H. Neale & Son had effectively come to an end. Charles had an arrangement with his friend and fellow dairyman, Tom Sheaf, which finished the business and ended half a century of the Neale family enterprise. This was also around the time that Burr Street, originally built in the middle of the nineteenth century and named after the brewing family, was finally earmarked for demolition and redevelopment. It is perhaps ironic that one of the first new buildings to be built across the road from number 13 Burr

Arthur Neale (BN)

Street in the newly developed Duke Street was a modern   mechanized dairy business – the new replacing the old! Nowadays numbers 13 and 15 Burr Street are the modern premises of the Headways Hat Company. Charlie and Louisa moved to Derwent Road when 13 Burr Street was demolished in 1955, and Charlie died in 1969, followed by Louisa a year later. Son died in Taunton Avenue in 1992. Barry, the fourth generation of Luton-born Neales to live in Burr Street (albeit for only six months in his case), still lives locally with his wife. Now retired from a career with the Ministry of Defence, Barry is a magistrate on the Luton and South Bedfordshire Bench.

Albert and Edwin Oakley came from a family of eight in their native Tottenham, London in 1875 and started their business in Luton. First they used a handcart, selling lard, cheese and bacon at street markets in Leighton Buzzard, St. Albans, Hemel Hempstead and in Luton by the Ames Memorial, known as the 'Pepper Pot', in front of the Corn Exchange. Business progressed and they soon expanded with a shop in Hitchin Road, replaced shortly after by 85 High Town Road, then considered to be a very smart part of town. Here they cleared away some old cottages and erected the first building of any note in this road. The back of the shop was used as a processing plant where the bacon was cut up, smoked and cured. The sides of bacon were cleaned and coated with peameal, which gave the rind a rich brown colour when hung above the smouldering sawdust overnight.

Albert walked up through the fields to where he built a substantial home at the apex of High Town Road and Hitchin

Road. Edwin lived at 'The Mount' in New Bedford Road. With business thriving, Albert and Edwin decided to open a second shop in Chapel Street. They built a pair of matching shops in 1900 on a site which was previously held by Henry Brown and his timber business. Number 8 was sold to the Rudd family for their confectionery and pastrycook business and number 6 became the quaint traditional style provision merchants remembered by so many people of Luton for so many years. Beautifully fitted, it boasted magnificent Victorian tiles in green, cream and gold around the walls and cornice. The wooden counters with their shining brass scales displayed the best in cooked meats and cheeses. In 1917 Albert sadly died when he was

Albert and Edwin Oakley (PO)

Oakley's stall, on the right, at the George Street market, 1925 (PO)

Oakley's had the best cooked hams in town. In the same year Edwin, the remaining founder, died, leaving William to run the firm. Always smartly attired and wearing his bowler hat, he visited his special wholesale customers every week to personally receive their orders. He called on Leighton Buzzard, Wing, Dunstable and Luton. Among his customers locally were Martins and Barringers in High Town Road, Charlie Jones in Park Street, Heddens in Court Road and Sammy Barrow in Buxton Road. William appointed a new Manager to Chapel Street in 1934 and Leonard Kingshott held that position for the next fifty years, living above the shop and ruling it firmly. The wrought iron sign at the top of this story could be

thrown from a pony and trap, and the following year his son William joined the family firm. Both shops continued to do well, with High Town concentrating on the wholesale market and Chapel Street on top quality provisions and table delicacies. At this time there were displays of Del Monte pilchards costing 6 ½ d. (3p) a tin, and the same brand of tinned salmon was 1/2d a tin. They advertised that they sold 'the breakfast bacon with a reputation', specially shipped from the factory and smoked in their own stoves daily. The public was asked to ' Try it and be satisfied'. A wider range of quality products were added to the Chapel Street display in 1930 such as Tiptree preserves, Cooper's Dundee marmalade, tinned and dried fruit, teas and quality food hampers. Sugar was weighed manually, cheese was always wire-cut to your satisfaction and of course

85 High Town Road (PO)

seen above the Chapel Street windows.

Lutonian Joan Cockfield joined Oakley's as Miss Kirton in 1943, straight from school at the age of 14, and stayed with them until after her marriage, and has many happy memories of her 21 years with them. She was employed at High Town Road as a Junior Clerk and progressed to Invoice Clerk. Her duties included processing the orders taken by the company representatives and invoicing them in triplicate, also completing the ledger, cash book and day book, of course all in longhand. Joan also made the tea, across the yard in the harness room, and recalls dressing the window from the pavement side. At this time Mr. Janes was the shop manager and Mr Harvey was the warehouse manager who lived above the shop on the first floor and he had a housekeeper, Mrs. Rowbotham.

During the war years the company struggled, like all traders, with lack of supplies and rationing. After WW2 a delivery service was introduced and an assistant Margaret Harris was employed to help Mr Kingshott. William's son Peter joined the company in 1951 and, when William died in 1970, Peter took over the running of the business and had a new frontage built with very recognizable bay windows. A coffee roasting machine was installed and the aroma of freshly ground

Interior of 6 Chapel Street (PO)

Leonard Kingshott and Peter Oakley   (PO)

coffee beans wafting down Chapel Street is remembered with pleasure by so many. The fuel crisis of this time made deliveries too costly to continue. When Mr. Kingshott retired, Margaret Harris took over the running of the Chapel Street branch. The family were forced to sell the High Town Road branch for council development in 1982 and this area is now the St. Matthew's Schools. At this point the wholesale business and offices were moved to Brooklands Farm in the Bedfordshire village of Greenfield, from where Peter and his son Jonathan still trade, supplying local butchers and grocers, pubs, restaurants, hotels and caterers. However, in 1993 the Chapel Street shop had a total refit, installing new counters and creating a kitchen for the sale of home-made sandwiches, baguettes and rolls. A further kitchen was added four years later to allow the shop to make its own pies. After 45 years service it was time for Margaret to retire and staff member June Bernard was appointed Manageress. She continued to develop home-made products but she too retired after 32 years with Oakley Brothers. In 2001, with profits falling, the family decided to close the Chapel Street shop. However an ex-butcher from Birdsfoot Lane in Leagrave endeavoured to make a success of it for a further eighteen months, but final closure came in June 2003. The clientele had changed, the old Luton families who had been their customers had gone, and parking near the shop became more difficult so, after 128 years in Luton, Oakley Brothers closed down. Number 6 Chapel Street is now Roosters chicken take-away.

The original entrepreneurs, Albert and Edwin, were active in local politics and both served as mayors of Luton. Albert in 1903 and Edwin on three occasions, in 1891, 1894 and 1906. Albert was

6 Chapel Street (PO)

withstanding any assault upon what he believed to be true". When he retired from the Council in 1920, he had been a member continuously for 37 years. In 1921 the freedom of the Borough was conferred on him in appreciation of his eminent services and although then giving up municipal work, Edwin Oakley continued to be an Alderman of the Bedfordshire County Council and a member of the Lee Conservancy Board. Some years later, in 1951, in fact 48 years after his father was mayor, the Oakley family's service to Luton council was renewed when William's brother Richard Charles was also elected mayor of Luton. In 1956 he became High Sheriff of Bedfordshire. Furthermore the original Oakley Brothers will be remembered for saving Wardown Park for the town, which at this time was known as Scargills. When the park was put up for sale at £17,000 in 1904, the council was reluctant to buy it. However Edwin Oakley, together with fellow council member Asher Hucklesby, stepped in and purchased it privately for £16,500. They later sold it back to the town for the same sum. Alderman John Burgoyne later described them as "prominent figures in that quiet but thriving little town, two sturdy men of great integrity, trusted by their townspeople as it is given to few to be trusted".

Chairman of the Luton Division Bench of Magistrates, Justice of the Peace for 29 years, Chairman of the Watch Committee for 25 years, Secretary of Luton Liberal Club for nearly 40 years and for some time a governor of Luton Modern Schools. He was said to have acted in public life "with insight, rectitude, wisdom and scrupulous impartiality" and in private life as well as public "he was a man of the highest integrity, not given greatly to speech but one whose word was as sacred as an oath. He was faithful to his convictions and solid as a rock in

ASHLEY OVERHILL

"A pleasant and nutritious substitute for food in travelling, or when unusual fasting is caused by irregular periods of meal times". It's surprising to know that this was the description given for eating-chocolate that appeared in Butler's Medicine Chest Directory in 1826. It is the earliest known reference in this country and was part of an advertisement for Fry's Chocolate Lozenges.

Sweet shops seem to be a vanishing breed! In these days of lines of plastic bins full of imported confectionery, which it is suggested we 'pic 'n' mix', the age of the wooden counter and the traditional glass bottles full of black jacks and gob stoppers is gone. Everyone has memories of the sweet shops of their childhood, indeed I lived at one. It was often a case of 'if I buy only one of these, maybe I can get something else and I wonder if the humbugs are better value than

Four generations of the Overhill family, Ashley is standing (SS)

the toffees!' Anyway we always got something mouth-wateringly sweet or unbelievably sticky, but always it was colourful. It didn't matter that Mum had warned 'they'll rot your teeth!' I think a little sugary name-dropping is called for here... do you remember Rainbow Crystals, Banana Toffee, Candy Shrimps, Midget Gems, Clover Rock, Sherbert Dabs, Aniseed Balls, Acid Drops, Silver Cachous, Flying Saucers and Liquorice Bootlaces? Don't forget the giant candy babies' dummies and the grinning sugar false teeth! Then we bought Murraymints, the 'too good to hurry mints', we 'tasted the cream' when every 1/2lb bar of Cadbury's Dairy Milk chocolate had 'a glass and a half of full cream milk' poured into it and Bertie Bassett was 'the sweetest friend of the family'.

For a few years in Luton's town centre, from 1953 in Upper George Street, we had just such a typical British sweetie shop which offered for sale all those delectable goodies we have learned to love. At number 32, between Alma

Ashley Overhill (SS)

Street and Lancret's Path and next to Booth's china shop, was the establishment of Mr. Ashley Overhill. He was born in 1891 in Hastings Street. His father, Henry, was a blockmaker in both wood and composition and also a native of Luton. His mother was of Scottish parents. When Ashley was two years old they moved house to 46 Regent Street. After Chapel Street school and York House private school, he joined his father at the age of 14, in the family business at 17a Adelaide Street. An enthusiastic swimmer, he could swim the full length of Wardown Park lake when he was 16 and became a member of the Luton Water Rats who each year celebrated Christmas by breaking the ice on the lake before a swim. In 1913 Ashley married Florence Hudson, daughter of Isaiah Hudson, the Leagrave coal merchant. They set up home at 25 Lyndhurst Road. World War One saw service in the Flying Corps and in peacetime Ashley returned to rejoin the family business of block and pan makers to the hat trade, moving it on four occasions later to 21 Chapel Street, 12 Church Street, Stanley Walk and back to 29 Church Street. He was now with a new partner, Mr Barton. During WW2 he was Head Air-Raid Warden for the South Bedfordshire area. In 1947 Ashley was elected Councillor with a good majority in the St. Mary's Ward of Luton and re-elected in 1951. As Chairman of the Parks & Entertainments Committee he had the pleasure of meeting H. M. The Queen and Prince Philip at the Town Hall and was also present at the luncheon given for the Rt. Hon. Sir Winston Churchill. He was also successful in gaining permission for the crematorium to be built at Stopsley. By now he had two sons, Ronald and Jack. Ronald was a hat manufacturer in Alma Street and lived above the factory. Ashley was living in Ludlow Avenue and the opening of his sweet shop was a surprising departure for he was now in his 60s. He bought it as a going concern from Mr Frederick Arnall.

The final stage of the de-rationing of sweets in February 1953 took place whilst Ashley was running his town centre sweet shop. The child with the Saturday penny who could get 2oz of sweets for that before the war could not buy many loose

Ashley's sweet shop was on the right in this photograph of Upper George Street

sweets for that in 1953. Not many were sold for less than 6d. a quarter. Generally the public seemed to prefer spending 3/- on a half-pound box of good chocolates rather than buying a larger quantity of cheaper sweets and Ashley specialised in boxes of chocolates. It was reported with astonishment in The Luton News that in one store a woman walked in and bought £1 worth of sweets! Ashley Overhill presided over his shop, selling cigarettes, tobacco and confectionery during the years when it once again became possible for us all to choose, to delight in, to indulge ourselves in the purchase of sweets and chocolate. Surely we all agree with Roald Dahl who said 'The joys of milk flakes, chew bars and energy balls are the stuff of dreams'. By 1957 his sweetie shop had become the offices of the Northampton Town & County Building Society and today it is rebuilt as Apex House. Ashley died in 1980 but Ronald and his wife are both 89 this year. His grand-daughter Sally still lives in Bedfordshire and is in charge of External Sales and Marketing for The Book Castle, the publishers of this book.

J. H. Page

John Page's public school education in Latin, French and Ancient Greek was hardly appropriate for his preferred career in engineering, let alone the purveying of carpets and floorcoverings. Having left University College School, London in 1931, he became apprenticed at Barkers Department Store, Kensington and pursued six years of servicing, installing and testing Royal Air Force aircraft engines during the Second World War before becoming commissioned in the RAF Regiment. In 1945, in Newcastle on Tyne, John married Nancy Miller who was serving in the WAAF. They eventually arrived in Luton in November 1951, John becoming Carpet Department Manager with Blundell Brothers. John had descended

John Page (JP).

from a family of farming entrepreneurs. However, on 9th July 1959 he opened his own carpet retailing business at 22 Chapel Street in the recently vacated premises of W. Bell & Sons, the bespoke tailors and outfitters. Nancy and John had three sons, John, Robert and David.

1959 was the tail end of the post-war boom and the run up to the MacMillan 'You've never had it so good' election – and so it proved. The business thrived, especially with the able assistance of Percy Woodley (a veteran of both World Wars), 'Scotty Scot' the carpet fitter (ex-RAF Lancaster wireless operator), Geoff Hampshire the mover (whose removal vans had the most attractive livery around Luton) and Herbert Pearce (Parachute Regiment and gentleman to the core). The firm's speciality was in the niche market of quality carpets. The tufted variety was looked on with disdain and it was primarily Wilton and Axminster carpets that were supplied. Squares were the order of the day at the start, but fitted carpets rapidly took over as the 60s progressed, the firm gradually progressing into curtains and other soft furnishings. Growth was enhanced with sustained advertising, culminating in a substantial campaign on the Luton Corporation red buses. On these they stated that they could supply carpets and floorcoverings, including vinyl, lino, cork and wood parquet tiles and also headboard casing. However quality carpets were their strength.

Page's advertisement on a Luton Corporation bus (JP)

There remained a very practical side to John Page; his interest in industrial archaeology through the Newcomen Society, model engineering and, in particular, live steam water-tube boilers. Frequently, all domestic activity would be sacrificed to tube bending, riveting, caulking and testing with ferocious gas burners. Performance was exceptional and superheated steam output prodigious. Mercifully, nothing ever exploded and all boilers remain in working order in the hands of younger enthusiasts. In complete contrast, before the Second World War, he had, like his father, been a fine shot and excellent horseman. In post-war austerity Britain, however, these were not easy interests to sustain with his late 40s nomadic life, and in any event re-establishment of his business life had to come first. Thus after periods in Brighton, East Devon and East Kent, John Page eventually settled in Luton; an excellent choice as he never moved on, the more cosmopolitan Bedfordshire

lifestyle suiting him well.

Before the arrival of the Arndale Centre, with the resultant shift in Luton's commercial centre of gravity, life in Chapel Street was bustling, with Gibbs and Dandy , Thomas Cook, Oakley Brothers, Partridges and The Griffin public house, which was the meeting place of the Luton Model Engineers, all adding to what was a congenial commercial centre.

Life frequently took an amusing turn. One day whilst a bank robbery was taking place at the Westminster Bank in George Street, Scotty the fitter found that his way through the business service road at the side of Partridge's was blocked by a ladder leading over the wall into Gibbs and Dandy's storage yard. In removing the ladder, he unwittingly denied the bank robbers their getaway route and indeed could have been the 'hero of the hour' in delaying them long enough for the police to intervene. Unfortunately, the news travelled slowly that day and, having passed the obstructed point, Scotty replaced the ladder against Gibbs and Dandy's wall and restored the getaway route. Thus the gang got clean away. There were to be no additional medals to those gained for his wartime service!

Nothing is for ever. As the 60s

22 Chapel Street   (JP)

birthday   It was 16 years to the day since it had opened. Thus came to an end an era which saw the woven carpet largely give way to the tufted alternative, the rise of the mass retailing of low cost fitted carpets and the movement of Luton's commercial life to east of George Street, with the disappearance of most of Cheapside and many of the businesses towards Guildford Street.

Following closure, the property was taken over by the Coal Advisory Centre and today is the newsagents, Hatters News. However, for the Page family, the whole enterprise was undoubtedly well worthwhile. Successful business is much more than just money, it is also about contributing to, providing quality service to, and being part of the community. Self well-being is much more than the self centred view of profit. John Page gained from, but also contributed considerably to, commercial life in Luton. He died in 1997, aged 81.

progressed, retail price maintenance, introduced as a post WW2 trading measure, was discontinued and life for small traders gradually became more difficult. Soon, carpet manufacturers discriminated, albeit from the pressure of bulk purchasing power, in favour of large carpet retailers – a move they would eventually come to regret. Whilst it was still commercially worthwhile remaining in the niche market of the quality carpet, the inflationary 70s and the increasingly bureaucratic nature of business life at that time made commerce progressively more difficult and eventually John Page reluctantly concluded that, as none of his three sons wished to continue the family business, it would close in 1975 on his 60th

The interior of 22 Chapel Street   (JP)

U. & F. PAMPALONI

I make no excuse for including this story for a purely personal reason. The subjects form part of my wife's family tree and we hope that possibly, just maybe, some elderly person reading this may recall their childhood in Luton's High Town, remember this family grocers and contact us. We would love to hear from them. We have found one charming lady who can do this and I will recall her memories shortly.

Until my mother-in-law married, Pampaloni was the family name and we have the records back through Sabatino, Carol-Pasquale, Lorenzo, Domenico and Giovanni to the sixteenth century when they were living in the wonderful Italian city of Florence. Four generations back my wife's great-great grandfather Luigi was a sculptor there and his work can be seen throughout the city and beyond in Empoli and Pisa. Statues adjacent to Florence cathedral and in Santa Croce and even Napoleon's bathroom in the Pitti Palace bear witness to his abilities. His home in the city centre bears a plaque recording this fact. Two generations later Ugo came to this country at an early age and later emigrated to New York where he worked as a clerk at an art gallery, the site of which is now under the Lincoln Centre. In America he met and married, at The Holy Trinity Church on Wall Street, a Geordie girl Frances Bass, who was working at the Glen Ridge Hotel in New Jersey. Frances was a niece of William Ross who was the landlord of The Britannia public house in Luton's Burr Street. They returned to this

Ugo, Frances and Dorothy Yolanda

country, living first at 101 Flood Street in Chelsea and then came to Luton to assist their relations at The Britannia. Ugo, who was generally known as Paul, entered the service of plait merchant Paolo Vincenzi at 21 King Street and remained there all his working life. In private life Ugo was an ardent Oddfellow, being a Member of the Loyal Victory Lodge of the Manchester Unity. On several occasions he held office as Noble Grand. He also served on the Management Committee of the Luton Medical Institute for many years and passed through the Chair. He was also a linguist of no mean ability, speaking French, German, Spanish and English as well as his native Italian. He spoke of and thought highly of the land of his adoption. The validity for this story in this book came about when they moved in 1912 to the shop at 79 Havelock Road, on the corner with Reginald Street, and Frances became the local grocer.

Miss Gladys Shortland, who is also mentioned herein as part of the Barrett's Garage story, lived with her parents at number 81 on the opposite corner. Gladys has colourful memories of her time there as a young girl of nineteen, recalling that the windows of most of the houses in the road had blinds edged with lace. The grocer's shop of F. E. Pampaloni, she calls to mind, sold "slices of ham and slices of bacon and lots of things for tuppence." She says, "the shop had two narrow doors but only one was ever opened so that nobody could get out with anything quickly or take anything off the counter, because they'd get stuck in the doorway. There was method in the madness."

Attending the services at nearby St. Matthew's church has remained firmly in her memory. She says the Pampaloni family regularly sat in a side aisle one row behind her own family. "They always came in the last couple of minutes just

The district meeting of The Manchester Unity of Oddfellows at Woburn in July 1922, Ugo is 3rd from right, centre row.

before the Vicar's family. I remember it distinctly." she said. "They were nice people, always looked just so, always correctly dressed, so distinguished. Frances always had such beautiful suits, dark grey or black and with cream or white blouses; and the hats!!... she had such beautiful hats with all the trimmings on. They used to go to town trimming hats in those days. We always knew when the Pampalonis came in, they always came in through a different door to us, like the Wernhers from the Hoo did at St. Mary's! I've heard the Vicar say 'We shan't start yet, the Pampalonis are not in!' It was a very big church and very full in my days."

Frances died in 1921, aged 61, and Ugo died only five years later, aged 66. The shop was occupied next by Mr Illesley and later by Mr Robinson, it remaining a grocer's for many years, but subsequently becoming a typewriter service company. Now converted to flats, the glass windowlight above the house door still bears the name of my wife's mother, Frances and Ugo's daughter, 'Yolanda'.

Havelock Road as it is today.

It was in 1892 that Daisy's lover, who could not afford a carriage, felt sure that she would look sweet on their bicycle made for two! Could it have been a New Hudson, I wonder, for shortly after this they were selling well through a shop remembered with affection by many Lutonians, namely Lloyd, Partridge & Co. at 10-12 Chapel Street. The New Hudson Company kept a warehouse there and "The New Hudson Cycle Depot" was proudly proclaimed right across the building above the first floor. In 1925 their products cost between £6.15.0 (£6.75) and £14.14.0 (£14.70) and they had a guarantee of fifteen years. But other brands were also stocked, such as Rudge-Whitworth and Raleigh, the all-steel bicycle which "kept the noiseless tenour of your way", and Lutonians could cycle away from Chapel Street after a first payment of ten shillings (50p). Partridge's were also sole agents for New Hudson motor cycles, the 35hp Semi-Sports cost £50, the Tourist model was £53, the 49hp TT Sports cost £55 and the OHV Super Sports sold for all of £60. Motor-cycle business was as important as the cycle section, for they were also agents for the sales of Royal Enfield, Royal Speedwell,

Sunbeam, Singer, Raleigh and BSA. I am sure many of us can recall ogling at the Hornby train sets and the dolls in their windows and in November queueing there for fireworks, and what a spectacular display they had on show. May I remind you of Magic Fountains, Empire Guns, Windmills, Bombshells, Parachutes, Flying Fleas, Black Jacks, Autogyros, Belisha Beacons and of course

Lloyd, Partridge in the 1920s (ES)

Partridge's shop in the 1930s   (ES)

the rockets and the sparklers. In 1930 they advertised Meccano sets from 2/- (10p), wooden train sets from 10/6, clockwork toys at 1/-, Hornby train sets from 5/- (25p), dolls' prams from 39/6 and their houses from 19/11. For 32/6 you could purchase the junior Chevrolet Regal Motor. The stock was extensive, for they also sold photographic, leather, fancy and Japanese goods, mail carts and portmanteaus and, as "The Complete Athletic Outfitter", everything for cricket, football, tennis, hockey and croquet as well as perambulators, games and toys.

In 1925 Harold Groves Partridge took complete control and the name above the overflowing windows became simply H. G. Partridge & Co. 'Partridge's' became the goal for all the youngsters of the town for many years. The thriving business was sold shortly after WW2 when it became the property of Mrs Joan Guyver, who received it as a wedding present from her husband, the owner of Guyver Trading at Tunbridge Wells. The company also had cycle and toy shops at Maidstone, Woking and Holloway in London. The motor cycle trade in Luton was shed at this time and toys, prams and nursery goods were introduced. The respected name of Partridge was retained above the shop.

Eric Sutton became Partridge's manager in November 1974. He had held managerial positions with Debenhams, Dickens & Jones and Beatties before coming to Luton to join Blundell's and later Eveling's. With Debenhams in his home town of Canterbury, Rev. Dr.

Shop interior showing the bicycle display   (ES)

Hewlett Johnson, known as The Red Dean, was a customer of his in the materials department, and Phyllis Calvert, Yvonne de Carlo, The Beverley Sisters and Edmundo Ros were his customers whilst at Dickens & Jones. During his 26 years in Luton, eventually completing his time here with the Belfast Linen Co., he was President of the Luton & District Chamber of Trade for two consecutive years. He is now retired in South Humberside.

Despite competitive trading by the Co-Op and Mothercare, Partridge's maintained a successful position in the town until 1979, when the offer made by The Bank of Ireland to buy the property was something that Mrs

Guyver could not refuse. After about 80 years Partridge's closed to business on 31st January 1980 and the Bank of Ireland still occupies this very old building.

Santa Claus visited Partridge's every Christmas

D. Pratt

I have placed D. Pratt at the heading of this page as it is the most prominent in the accompanying 1955 photograph used here. Although the story concerns all of them, it seems to be the most well-remembered of the 'temporary' shops built by the local council at this location.

The Farley Hill estate was built as part of the clearance plan of condemned housing in the town. The first houses built were allocated to residents of Elizabeth Street, Hastings Street and New Town Street. It was an extensive estate, built on a pleasant grassy landscape over which I used to roam with my grandparents and which we always knew as 'the lynces'. I took photographs there as it was being developed, one of which, in Santingfield North, is seen here. The new residents of this estate were in urgent need of some local shops, those in the town centre being considered too far away to use. Later the town bus turned round at the roundabout by the shops. In about 1948, the council's solution was to build these six simple shops which were supposed to be temporary, but were in use for quite some time, indeed until Market Square was built. They were constructed on the edge of Whipperley Ring facing down Whipperley Way and they remained busy until the early 60s. Most of the area behind them was still open landscape. Now there are flats built there and The Parrot public house.

Nearest to the camera in our picture is the newsagent's shop run by David Pratt who, with his father and mother, also ran another similar shop near the corner of Chapel Street and New Street. They also owned the corner shop which they rented out to a barber. Long before the temporary shops were built, David's father, Dick, had started delivering newspapers on the new Farley Hill development. The posters on the newsboards outside the shop are noteworthy. That for the local Tuesday newspaper 'The Pictorial' advertises that it has the full report on the football match between Luton Town and Burnley. This was played on September 5th 1955 and took place in Division I. Gordon Turner scored for Luton, but

The temporary shops, 1955

they lost 3-1.
Another poster
mentions the late
Gilbert Harding,
the famous
broadcaster, who
was writing for
'The Daily Sketch'
at the time.

When he was a
boy, David Franks,
who is now a
councillor and
currently

Santingfield North under construction, c1950

leader of the local council, did an evening newspaper round for the Chapel Street shop after school, which was Surrey Street Secondary Modern. His parents had moved to Luton from the north-east and hoped that one day they may be able to move from Regent Street and live on the council estate, where the houses had running hot water and inside toilets, but they were not successful in doing so. Pratts are advertising Players, Capstan and Churchill No.1 cigarettes outside their premises and on their windows. Peter Bodsworth of Barnfield Avenue remembers how he loved going into their shop to buy sweets. Jamboree Bags were the big craze in those days. Peter is the six year old little boy in the baggy trousers, on the right of the group of three children in the photograph. Behind them can be seen the Lyons Bread van making its delivery, a familiar sight around the town. Mrs Shirley Hobbs of Meyrick Avenue lived as Miss Thompson for thirteen years in The Crossway nearby,

before she was married. Pratt's has special memories for her as she used to walk there most Saturday evenings to buy the local Sports Telegraph, known as the 'Green'Un'. Those were the days before most people owned television sets, so the football paper was bought hot off the press after 6.30pm, people often queueing for it to learn the day's results. She says 'I wish it could make a comeback!'

The Luton Industrial Cooperative Society traded in two of the 'huts', being the local grocer and the local butcher. Other traders here were R.A.Hopkins who were the chemists and who also ran the Post Office counter, Mr Rhodes who started as the Kandy Shop but was a grocer later on, and Mr Rayment was the greengrocer. Pratt's moved into no.2 Market Square, the more permanent premises when they were built, but David could often be heard remarking that he was doing no more business there than he did in the 'hut'.

GEORGE RIPPER
HAIRDRESSER

Did you know that Lord Ripper was related to Howard Carter? … If you didn't, read on! …

In the well preserved Norfolk Georgian town of Swaffham, several generations of the Ripper family lived in a farmhouse which dated from 1717. They believe that their ancestors had sailed from Austria into Kings Lynn, which many Austrians had done at that time. James Benjamin Ripper, who lived to be 94, had a son, John Thomas Ripper, who made a living making shoes and riding boots, also by keeping bees and selling the honey to the residents of Swaffham. John married Amelia Beatrice Carter, also of the town, and together they had six children, alternating boys and girls – Marguerite,

George, Mary, John, Catherine and Benjamin. Amelia's father and Howard Carter's father were brothers, so our subject George was second cousin to the brilliant archaeologist who is most remembered for his discovery of the tomb of Tutankhamen in 1922.

Howard Carter was a Swaffham boy whose father was an enthusiastic collector of Egyptian antiquities and George's youngest brother Ben remembers him well. He recalls Howard returning to his home town following the discovery in Egypt and giving a talk at the local cinema. Ben jokingly says that at the time he thought it was about Tooting Common! It was good to visit Ben, who is 88 and now living on his own in the family house in Swaffham. He has been a town councillor; in 1979 he wrote a local history book of Swaffham titled "Ribbons From the Pedlar's Pack" and is also a very successful artist, one room of his home being given over entirely to his paintings of local scenes.

As a boy George was inventive, spending a lot of time making his own phonograph. He recorded the family and even the Town Band on its cylindrical drum. He left school at 14 but sadly his relationship with his father was not congenial. However he did stay to serve a four years apprenticeship with local barber Charlie Hawkins. As soon as he was 18 he left home

George's shop at 63 Stuart Street

and came in our direction, working for a hairdresser in Hemel Hempstead. His next move was to Luton, where in 1931 he set up in his own gent's hairdressing business at 63 Stuart Street. It was a busy place, with four chairs and room for about 7 or 8 persons to wait their turn. George's brother John also worked in the business. During WW2 George did his duty as a "special" in the local police force.

Ripper's (what an unfortunate name for a hairdresser!) remained busy here until 1964 when the Stuart Street dual carriageway was built, and the foundations are now under the newer side of the road, adjacent to the Magistrates Court. George moved his business up to 115 Wellington Street, on the corner with Dumfries Street, where he now added sales of fishing tackle and bait. This is now the premises of Sounds Authentic. In his spare time George was an accomplished magician and card manipulator, giving many shows to local audiences. He was also an enthusiastic amateur photographer and cinematographer, filming many civic

Phyllis and George Ripper (CB)

events in the town. His films were later transferred to video and sold under the title of "Luton Celebrates". Together with his Irish wife Phyllis they lived at 95 London Road and they had one adopted son, John. George lived to a good age, dying in 2000, aged 94.

Oh ... I haven't explained about Lord Ripper. Well, John Thomas Ripper believed that his children would have a better chance in life with more dignified Christian names than is usual. So Mary was christened Princess Mary and our local barber really was Lord George Ripper!

M. P. Rudd & Sons, Ltd.

Pastrycooks and Confectioners

Pat-a-Cake, Pat-a-Cake, Baker's Man, Bake Me a Cake as fast as you can … in our town the Rudd family baked cakes as fast as they could for eighty years.

The founder, William Rudd, was born in St. Albans in 1843 and came to Luton as a boy. However at the age of 18 he returned to his birthplace, where he served an apprenticeship in Alfred Cole's bakery in the Market Place at St. Albans. About 1868 he returned to Luton where he had relatives in the trade, founding his confectionery and pastrycook business by living and opening a shop at 42 George Street, later occupied by plait merchants J.J.Linsell & Co. This would have been on the site currently occupied by the present Marks & Spencer building. William had by now married Elizabeth Powell. They had two sons, William jnr in 1871 and Frank in 1872. Within twelve months William had closed this shop and decided to try his luck in Australia, taking with him his wife and two sons and remaining there for two years. On return to England they set up home at Ashford in Kent, again with a bakery, but sadly Elizabeth died there at the age of 35. However, William soon remarried, this time to Suffolk girl Mary Polly Farthing. They continued the

8 Chapel Street, c1905

business in Kent but returned once again to Luton, re-establishing themselves here about 1885. Together with Mary, William had four more children, Bert, Phyllis, Ivy and Charles. All of his sons were to be involved in the family business.

Back in Luton they first opened at 24 Cheapside as The Central Coffee House, later at 57 Bute Street, and in 1901 they were living with their children and trading at 30 Chapel Street. A later more permanent move was to 8 Chapel Street, between Oakley Brothers and Lloyd, Partridge & Co. Edwin and Albert Oakley had built numbers 6 and 8 Chapel Street in 1900 and sold number 8 to the Rudd family. Although they had four children and despite the apparent prosperity in business, the marriage was not a success. At some point after this Mary Polly, supported by son Bert, threw William out of the family home! I quote present descendents when I say "William was not a nice man, he had a foul temper, was a womaniser and could get violent on a relatively small amount of alcohol".

This eventually led to a legal separation.

After this Mary Polly, together with William jnr, Bert (who had up to now been a carpenter) and Charlie formed M. P. Rudd & Sons. Frank joined later but always had a smaller share than the others and left them after WW1 to set up in business on his own, being recalled for emergency bakehouse service during flu outbreaks. For another fifty years the three branches of 8 Chapel Street, which was by far the largest (now the Efeler Kebab Takeaway Restaurant), 71 Park Street (near the junction with Lea Road), where the bakehouse for all branches was next to the shop, and 164 Dunstable Road (now Time & Sonic) continued very profitably. Bert, who was in charge of the office and administration side, had a very strong character and played an influential part, taking charge after the death of Charlie and eventually being the survivor of the original partners. Avis, a shopgirl at Chapel Street, also joined the family firm when she married the boss's son Bert. Avis and Bert lived at the Dunstable Road branch which they had

(l to r) The founder William, Mary Polly and Bert Rudd (CR)

opened up just before their marriage. After WW2 a fourth shop was opened in Harpenden.

Joyce Findlay, who still lives in Luton, has pleasant memories of her years working for Rudd's. She felt at the age of 18, when jobs were few and far between, that she had attained a position of distinction, such was the good name of this company. She worked first in Dunstable Road and later in Park Street where Bert's daughter Beatrice was in charge. Munitions work at Skefko intervened during WW2 when long queues for bread would form at all bakers. Strict hygiene is a memory which remains with her, cleaning windows and shelves at the close of each day, the hosepiped bakehouse swimming in water every Saturday, and even scrubbing the drain covers. A job every Monday morning was to wash and polish the large glass barrels before displaying biscuits in them in a decorative pattern. Rudd's regarded themselves as pastrycooks and bread was a sideline. William jnr had first baked bread for family and friends, but it was placed on sale after customers had seen it and requested it. Pork pies, noted for their quality, pastries and also sliced cooked ham were sold. Rudd's name however was

Frank Rudd   (CR)

built on the wonderful quality and choice of their cakes, especially for the Wedding Day. Joyce recalls with relish their marzipan fruits, their very full cream buns, the chocolate éclairs and chocolate sprinkled fancies, huge cream-filled swiss rolls, sponges with three traffic-light coloured inlaid jam spots on top, and charlotte russe in which jelly and cherries stirred into stiffly whipped cream filled a mould of savoy or finger biscuits… mmm! Every weekend, and especially at Christmas time so that the pies and pastries were fresh, the master bakers would start work at 4 am and the shop staff would commence their day only an hour later. On Good Friday thousands of hot-cross buns would be baked for the three branches, which closed as soon as they were gone, nothing else being sold on this Holy Day. There were hundreds of "out of this world" cakes and at Christmas every staff member would receive one free. Rudd's was a thriving and prosperous business in Luton for about eighty years, but after the death of Bert the descendents were not enamoured with 4 am starts, so the company finally closed and was sold in 1967.

Mary Polly was a remarkable woman,

who treated her stepchildren on exactly the same terms as her own and they loved her for it. In her retirement she lived at 216 Leagrave Road, often using a carriage-built bath chair. She died in March 1935, aged 83, with her children and stepchildren about her. Bert died in 1965, aged 81. William, Mary, Phyllis and Ivy are buried in the General Cemetery in Rothesay Road, Luton. Frank umpired for Luton Town C.C. from 1905 until the outbreak of WW1. On returning to Luton he first umpired for the Wednesday XI, but finding it too demanding became their 1st XI scorer until his death. He was killed with his grandson Peter when a V2 rocket struck Biscot Road, Luton, on 6th November 1944. The war memorial by the Town Hall records the deaths of Frank Rudd, Colin Rudd and Peter Wise.

The founder, William Rudd, who died in June 1930, aged 86, became very frail and lived his later years at 'Downside', a boarding house/care home on Bradgers Hill, Luton. He was the founder of the Luton Social Club & Institute and had been the club's steward, secretary and treasurer. He helped form the local branch of the Bricklayers' Union and was chiefly responsible for the founding of a secular society in the town. He was also one of the original members of the Liberal Club. His funeral was a secular one, conducted by a Mr Rosetti. His "Luton News" obituary describes him more formally than his descendents, saying "he was a man who held strong views, especially in secular matters and was never afraid of expressing them".

The Normans' wedding cake, supplied by Rudd's

E. SANDERSON & SON LTD.

Bury Park Beer, Spirit & Wine Stores

Three hundred years ago the Bishop of Gloucester was attributed with the saying "Those who drink beer will think beer". Surely a saying which fits our subject, for he was a publican before he introduced his well remembered wine and spirit stores to Luton.

Frederick George Sanderson was born in Battersea, London, in 1878 and when old enough helped in a local restaurant. He married Gertrude Parcell, who was three years his junior, and moved into our area at "The Engineer" public house in Harpenden. He had followed his father into this profession, for he had also been a publican as licensee of "The Leviathan" in Watford. Gertrude, who was always known as "Auntie Gran", had three children, Eric, Maida and Mary, whilst they lived in Harpenden. They moved to St.Albans in 1911 and to Luton two years

later when they purchased the grocery shop at 15 Waldeck Road, on the corner with Bury Park Road, from the previous grocer W. Pestell. Their fourth child Louise was born here in 1918.

The grocery business was continued and off-licence business introduced. This meant they could sell any product and not be beholden to a given company. Frederick became a member of the Off-Licence Association of Luton & District in 1913. This local branch of the National Federation had been formed in 1894 when, for the sake of business stability, resolutions were passed fixing retail prices of the products they were selling. As business increased it became necessary in 1925 to ask a Mr Ashten to make alterations to increase the shop area. In 1938 Gertrude and Frederick moved their home to 16 Manton Drive when he was more able to enjoy his interest in golf. Their son Eric who had started work at the shop around 1918, married Marjory Alice White at Christ Church in 1929 and bought a house in

Frederick, Eric and Brian Sanderson (MS)

Bishopscote Road for which they paid £600. Their children Brian and Molly were born here. When Eric's parents moved out of the shop premises, however, Eric and Marjory moved in to live at the shop and remained there for the next fifteen years, where their second son Ian was born. The family tree includes two nationally known names: the antiquarian and archaeologist Worthington George Smith who lived in Dunstable and Luton artist Brian White whose cartoon strip "Nipper" was serialised in national newspapers.

Upon entering the shop the customer was confronted with a fine 18ft long mahogany counter, behind which were shelves displaying a wide range of wines,

15 Waldeck Road in 1960 (MS)

Inside the shop with (l to r) Paul Sanderson, Maisie Brooks, Brian Sanderson and David Lloyd (MS)

spirits and beer for consumption off the premises. The locally made beer from J.W.Green was sold and other popular beers such as Whitbread and Double Diamond which came from London by lorry and also Mackesons Stout and Guinness which their doctor would have recommended to them for good health! One had to be selective with the whisky, for there were 400 different varieties on the market. Everything in the shop was to hand, Anjou Rose to Yugoslav Reisling, 40 year old port, champagnes, liqueurs, Woodpecker cider, cigars and Mars bars. There was one lady customer who regularly removed the bottle crown caps with her teeth! Behind the scenes there was a storehouse with two floors. The lower floor housed the delivery van and

also cases of beer and cider, except for one corner which had a large double trapdoor into the upper floor. Upstairs stored fine wines, which were packed in wooden cases and protected and insulated with straw. Above the trapdoor was a large wooden beam, through which passed a heavy-duty hook from which was suspended a large chain and block and tackle. It was used to lift up to this floor the hogsheads of wine and there were usually three being processed at any time. Once there they were rolled onto a very sturdy wooden rack and wedged either side to ensure that they were safe. At the other end of the room was a sink for bottle washing and a rotary brush for cleaning the insides. After three or four days, when the barrels had had time to settle, they would be broached with a wooden tap which had to be knocked in with one mighty strike from a heavy mallet. There was no second chance with a pressure of fifty gallons of imperial wine there! After bottling the Australian and South African wines and corking, they were labelled and a foil cover pressed onto the top of the bottle. All back breaking work!

When WW2 was declared it was bad news for Sanderson's. The van could no longer be used for delivery of groceries and wine and they felt that the introduction of food rationing meant the end of the grocery side of the business. Also there was now a very limited supply of wines, beers and spirits available, but regular customers were assured of getting their order. As there was no real garden at the shop it was not possible to have an Anderson air-raid shelter, so a Morrison shelter was installed in the dining room. This had a four inch angle iron frame and a top of heavy gauge steel, it being used as a dining table or for table-tennis in the daytime. However, a mattress was placed underneath and during an air-raid the whole family would squash in and sleep underneath.

After the war, business expanded again, offering free glass loan and free delivery. Frederick died in 1947 but Eric was joined by his son Brian. He had been educated at Luton Grammar School and worked full time in the shop after demobilisation from National Service. Brian married local girl Margaret Greenwood at St.Andrews Church in 1954. Employed at various times were Bernard Willis, Bess Custance, Tony VanDyke and Maisie Brooks who was secretary and shop assistant. Also family members Grace, Maida, Louise and Dennis Lloyd who was Molly's husband. In the 1960s the shop was supporting four families. Opening hours were 10am to 2pm and 6pm to 10pm with Wednesday evening off. Between 2pm and 6pm there would be a rush to restock the shop. The Christmas season was very hectic. After closing time and a break for supper, Brian and friends would be working until 1.30am, restocking the shop and preparing the orders for delivery in the morning, especially when you realise that all the stock had to be trucked out of the store and in through the front door of the shop where there were often queues forming. In the evening the queues would sometimes stretch sixty feet down Waldeck Road as far as the Windsock Model Shop. Extra family and friends helped during December. Cousin Frank White, Peter Sharpe and Tony Roylance would come in after their regular work and help from 6pm to 11pm, followed by a lively get-together! Before the arrival of an electronic cash register and decimalisation, mental calculations were difficult, often requiring the cost to be written down on the wrapping paper, for instance six pints of Whitbread beer, times one shilling and elevenpence halfpenny! One thing difficult to realise today is that beers and minerals came in wooden crates and the bottles were returned by the customers, 6d for quart empties and 3d for pint empties and they all had to be returned to the correct crates as there were at least five different brewers involved. The back yard became cluttered with crates stacked like skyscrapers and it was often Easter before the yard was clear of them. Brian became owner/manager on the death of his father Eric in 1973. Brian and Margaret lived at the shop for 24 years, their four children being born there, including their son Paul whose own son was also born there, so five generations of the Sanderson family had lived there before the shop closed down. In 1972 they advertised "A different bottle of wine weekly without (pardon!) repeating, we could accommodate you for about six years!" Bottle prices then were 68p for Anjou Rose, 83p for Piesporter, 64p for a Yugoslav Riesling and 69p for Mateus Rose. Sadly Brian died at the age of only 63 in 1994.

The Bury Park shopping area was a good place to shop. Ian Sanderson recalls that there was a bakery, a great model shop, Waller's the butchers, Stubbs' fish and chips, Chamberlain's hardware, Rudd's cake shop, Gunton's cut hair for a shilling, radio, corsets, milk, chocolate, newsagents, pet shop, bike shops and banks were all side by side. However economic conditions became more difficult across the country in the 70s and 80s, with liquor licences being granted to supermarkets and many other shops. This, together with the abolition of resale price maintenance, changed the face of business for the Sandersons. This fine old-style wine and spirit stores that had remained basically unchanged, for there was only Greener's in Stuart Street and Worlds End in New Town Street that were similar, closed on September 10th 1994 after 81 years. The oldest bottle left on the shelf was a 1927 port and the last one sold was a bottle of champagne. Daughter Molly lives in Dereham, son Ian is with his family in Rhode Island in the USA and Brian's wife Margaret remains with us in Luton. Daughters Rosalind and Heather live in Dunstable and Luton respectively, Paul is in Cornwall and Avril in Leeds. Margaret has eight grandchildren. Number 15 Waldeck Road is now occupied by Essex Illuminated Ceilings Ltd. but the renowned Sandeman Port & Sherry sign remains outside to remind us all of its popular past.

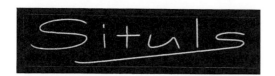
Of the one hundred stories of local entrepreneurs that I will have researched and written by the time this book reaches publication, this surely can be like no other. Whilst the majority of our subjects were either born Lutonians, in some cases almost two centuries ago, or else came here as young men or women, this story begins in Gujarat.

On the western Arabian Sea coast of India, Gujarat is a widely fertile plain on which cereals and cotton were grown, but is now highly industrialised. Here in the 1920s Tejshi Mulji Shah and his wife Monghiben were successful and affluent by any standards. However, they emigrated to Kenya for an even better future. Here in Nairobi Tejshi Shah built up and successfully operated coffee and pineapple farms. Tejshi also sponsored many Indian families in their move to Kenya and also from Kenya to England. Entrepreneur is surely an insufficient word, but there's more! In Nairobi they had nine children; the girls were Lalita, Ranjan, Vasanti and Nita, whilst the boys were Chandu, Amu, Mahendra, Ashok and Dinesh. In 1968, when there were political problems in Kenya, part of the family moved on again, this time to Wood Green in Greater London, for they were all holders of British passports.

Amu and Mahendra Shah's story was a great success. However the tragedy of the deaths of their father and elder brother Chandu pushed the family into a life of hardship and struggle. Mahendra was the first into British retailing when he took a stall in Kensington market, selling ladies' wear and silk scarves. Sheer hard work, vision and business intelligence paid off for the Shah brothers when they founded and opened gift shops in Wembley Arcade, Croydon and Wood Green, trading under the name of Sonya.

Kenyan community gatherings were held near their homes and it was at one of these that daughter Vasanti met her future husband who had also

Mahendra and Amu   (VS)

The display in the final shop at 51 Arndale Centre (VS)

been born in Kenya. In Nairobi he had been working in his uncle's clothing and gift shop. Chandrakant Sumaria and Vasanti were married in Finchley in 1972. They worship within Jaina, an ascetic Indian Hindu faith which dates back at least as far as 850BC and is related to and older than Buddhism. It is quite usual within this faith to use a different surname and Shah is a Hindu community name, so together with Chandrakant's

usual shortening of his first name, I am pleased to say that from herein we will know him as Chand Shah.

Chand worked with the Post Office at London's Mount Pleasant office for ten years whilst Vasanti was learning the retail gift trade at the Wembley and Wood Green shops on Saturdays, together with her full time job at a merchant bank in London. In 1978 Amu brought the family's flourishing, plentiful displays of myriad gifts to Luton in the shop we came to know as Situl's. Now we can all know why this name was chosen. Situl is the name of Mahendra's son. Vasanti and Chand also came to Luton at this time to work in the Situl shop, and they lived in Bramingham Green. In 1983 they set up home in Homerton Road where they live to this day with their two sons, one of them having been born there. The first of the three Situl shops in Luton Arndale Centre was in the main mall next to C & A. which is now Wilkinsons. This, their first shop next door, is now occupied by BodyCare. A move was later made to a side mall and finally, in 1997, to number 51, which is now Gregg's. At first frames, pictures and chess sets were specialised in, but this extended to tableware, vases, indeed the entire gift trade of novelties and collectable items. Copper products were imported from Zambia, but the majority of the stock originated in the Far East. A ready eye had to be kept on the changes in public demand, for the stock being imported was quite enormous as the Shah empire expanded. Bedford branch was opened in 1982. Chatham, Southampton, Nottingham, Manchester, Swindon, Reading, Watford, Southampton, Southend, Mansfield, Brent Cross and more followed, fifteen branches in all. Sadly in 1983 Amu died aged only 38 and since then four of the five brothers have died at an early age. The family firmly believe that this was caused by stressful working seven days a week. Only Ashok remains, now managing the Wood Green shop. This and the Bedford branch, which is managed by Ranjan and her husband Kanti, are now the only two remaining. The Watford branch is owned by Amu's son Ansu.

Chand and Vasanti Shah   (VS)

In March 2003 Situl's Gift Shop, one of the oldest independent traders in Luton Arndale Centre, was forced to close due to a drop in trade over the previous few years, but mostly due to an overflooded gift trade and the inability to cope with the spiralling overheads which come with being in the Centre. Surely the most valued gift Vasanti and Chand Shah gave us was bringing their popular shop to Luton for 26 years.

E. SPALDING
Hosiery and Lingerie Specialist

Corsets with whalebones, woollen stockings, art silk knickers, ladies combinations in pure wool, aprons, blouses, cardigans, hosiery, nightwear, gloves and all manner of undergarments. All this and so much more that women needed to make them look and 'feel' better. Everything except outdoor wear was available at Edith Spalding's little shop in Dunstable Road.

Three generations back, Thomas Spalding was a cowman. His son Bertram was a milkman in Rotherhithe where, in 1894, he married Emma Hubert whose father was a labourer. Bertram and Emma came to live at 206 Hitchin Road, Luton and he was employed at the British Gelatine Works. Edith Ellen Spalding (known to family and friends as Nell) was one of their family of five children. Edith had always wanted to own her own shop and before WW2 had been a buyer at ladies' outfitters Strange's in Wellington Street. No doubt she became inspired by this reputable business, which was founded by George Strange in 1832 and which traded in Luton for over a century. In 1935 Edith's dream came true when she opened her ladies' wear shop at 207 Dunstable Road midway between Ivy and Beech Roads, no doubt choosing this property as offering a good site for trade and also living accommodation suitable for her needs. Her widowed mother and her sister Winifred, who had also worked

at Strange's, lived with her. Dunstable Road at this time was the secondary shopping area after the town centre and many thriving businesses were nearby. Jack's the Tailor was next door, then a cooked meat shop and the confectioner and tobacconist was on the corner and simply called The Corner Shop. In the other direction there was Durrant's the butchers, A.C.River's furniture shop, Tudor Bakeries was nearby and on the other corner was Sinfield's the greengrocer.

Edith's shop was fitted out with glass cabinets and shelves and a central glass counter in which pretty blouses were always displayed. Stock was meticulously folded away in glass-fronted drawers which were all labelled with the correct

Edith Spalding (JBu)

price. The effective, but crowded, window display was neatly arranged, immaculately feminine and full of the characters of the ladies who presented it. All the items on show would have been ironed in the living room behind the shop and many items had their hand-written price tickets sewn on. Handkerchiefs were priced to the nearest farthing, in fact many items were priced to the odd three-quarters of a penny, for example 'elevenpence, three-farthings' or 'nineteen shillings and 11 3/4d'. Many shops offered a sheet of pins instead of the farthing change. Gloves were on sale only when Edith had managed to acquire some yarn and, together with her mother and sisters Winifred and Mabel, had crocheted them for sale. Mabel also ran her own credit drapery business. Silk stockings, when they could get them, were kept for favoured customers. Clothing coupons had to be taken from customers and counted during the war, and black-out during the winter nights meant putting wooden shutters over the window and using two sets of curtains at the shop door. At the end of each day the money in the till was counted and the till-roll on which every sale had been entered was swiftly added up. If there was even a penny missing, a great hunt ensued until Miss Spalding was satisfied that everything balanced and

207 Dunstable Road with (l to r) Marie Spalding, Joyce Wood and Edith Spalding (JBu)

was in perfect order.

Assistants Vera Dilley, Con Lawrence, Joyce Wood and Marie Spalding worked at the shop at various times, especially during the war years when Winifred was called to help the war effort at the local Skefko Ball Bearing factory. Marie started helping her Auntie on Saturdays when she was nine years old. She recalls catching the bus from Park Square, always carrying a small case containing one rasher of bacon, one egg and some sugar. This was her dinner which Gran cooked for her. Another memory is going with Aunt Nell to buy stock at the London warehouses of Pawsons & Leafs and Cooks of St.Pauls. She often had to pick her way through rubble from air-raids of the previous night to the sandbagged doors which no longer contained any glass. Marie helped out on Saturdays until she left school, when she joined Blundell Brothers. Joyce Hymus (nee Wood) helped from the age of 14 when, with her mother, they had called in to buy some gloves and was surprised to hear her mother ask if there was a job for her daughter. She commenced straight away and was for some time referred to strictly as Miss Wood. However, she did eventually become 'one of the family' and was often invited into the living room behind the shop for strawberries and cream. Joyce recalls that one of her duties was to stitch tickets onto all the lisle and plaited stockings showing the size and price. Monday morning's job was to dust the fixtures and all the underwear boxes, and of course the pavement was swept every morning.

Small shops like Miss Spalding's may have been less fashionable than the department stores, but they were more friendly than the bigger shops with their often imposing assistants. For 25 years Edith offered this friendly helpful service to the ladies of Luton. In 1959 she retired and moved home to Marsh Road in Leagrave when Winnie Mardle purchased the business and continued the service. Edith died in 1967, aged 69, and the shop is now Kashmir Stores.

J. A. STURTON Ltd.

The elegant building in Manchester Street, Luton, which stands between Gordon Street and Lancrets Path has, through the years, housed many different businesses. There have been estate agents, gents outfitters, sports goods dealers, ladies hairdressers, a casement curtain and blind specialist, even Luton Marriage Guidance Council and, after rebuilding in 1915, the WW1 recruiting office. However, one which lasted more years than most in this busy position was J.A.Sturton Ltd. who traded as ironmongers and hardware dealers for

Bill Bottrill (PB)

about thirty years. They were at number 33, which is now part of Sadler's Bar and Café.

J.A.Sturton Ltd. had its head-office at 19/21 Fitzroy Street in Cambridge. They had been a reputable company here since 1887, Richard, David and Joseph Sturton being proprietors over the years. Originally they were classed as chemists, oil merchants and grocers but by 1913 they had added microscopical, chemical and scientific apparatus to their sales, also having a china, glass and earthenware warehouse. Photographic dealing was added in 1927. Joseph was responsible for the development of much of the area between Newmarket Road and Mill Road in Cambridge which became known locally as Sturton Town. There were branches in Norwich, Lowestoft, Ipswich, Colchester, Great Yarmouth, Northampton, Edmonton and Ilford in addition to that in Luton. The manager of the Luton branch for many years and who held his job dear to his heart, was William Charles Bottrill who was born in Clifton-Upon-Dunsmore, Rugby, in Warwickshire. His first job, at the age of 14, was with hardware dealers Mence-Smith in Northampton but he later joined J.A.Sturton who also had a hardware shop in the same town. Whilst on holiday relief at their Lowestoft branch, he met Dorothy Turner who was to become his wife. In 1927 he was appointed manager of the Luton shop and in the first year received a praising letter from head-office congratulating him on his window display. The directors felt that it would certainly bring an increase in business. His salary at this time was based on 2.5% of the shop takings plus an annual bonus. Three years later Bill and Dorothy were married at Christ Church in Luton and lived at 140 Bishopscote Road. In 1936 they were able to watch a new home being built in what was then mostly fields and they were the first owner-occupiers in Alder Crescent, at number 97. One day in 1939 Bill heard Winston Churchill on the wireless making an appeal for people to join the Local Defence Volunteers which later became the Home Guard. Suitably impressed, he cycled straight to Luton Town Hall and became the first volunteer to do so in Luton. He was stationed in Leagrave, and having been issued with a rifle and a round of ammunition, kept watch on Leagrave Marsh in case the Germans parachuted in. He had to leave his job at the shop which he loved so much when he was called up to serve with the 1st Regiment of the Royal Horse Artillery, eventually fighting up through Italy under the command of Captain Hartley (of the Hartley Jams family). He was entitled to four medals in 1945 but did not claim them. In addition the war had brought him into a personal

The busy Sturton shop can be seen in Manchester Street (PB)

breakdown. On return to civilian life he applied to Sturton's to reclaim his old job but the firm had been taken over and the prospects were not as good with the new owners. He was very sad at this situation and reluctantly joined Vauxhall Motors, but did stay with them for 25 years. He and Dorothy had three children, Monica, Billy and Pat and the girls are still living in Luton. Bill was a conscientious and hard working man of quiet temperament who loved his garden and the countryside. He died in 1984.

He always spoke of his happy times at Sturton's in Manchester Street where to support him he had two young girl assistants and a delivery boy using a bicycle. The stock was varied and provided almost everything needed for the home. His children can still recollect most of it – stone hot-water bottles, candles, paraffin lamps and the necessary paraffin, brooms, dusters, linoleum, paints and whitewash, loose sugar and salt, condensed milk and tinned foods, tea in tinfoil-lined tea chests from which it was scooped into paper pockets for sale, tin baths, white enamelled bins with 'Bread' printed on them, bathroom accessories including enamel soap dishes in cream and green, wooden clothes pegs, seeds and metal watering cans, sand and cement, cream butterware crockery, saucepans, vinegar and bundles of firewood. Vinegar was in short supply when the builders of the nearby Alma Cinema fell behind their deadline with the wall plastering and used all the vinegar that Sturton's could supply to help dry it out more speedily. They advertised "We have potted meats, fish pastes, luncheon meats, also Marmite and Oxo for those party sandwiches. Also glasses, water sets, cake tins, meat tins, saucepans and frying pans. For cleaning we can satisfy your requirements". Bill would sharpen broom handles and assemble the brooms. The long wooden counters displayed all types of nails and the paper cone-shaped bags in which to sell them that Bill used to make himself. Indeed it was the forerunner of the modern DIY store. The stock always spilled over onto the pavement outside and it could take up to an hour to display it each morning, and the evening job when closed was to sprinkle sand on the wooden floor before watering it and sweeping up. His children remember with enthusiasm the fun they had carefully descending the ladder down into the large basement which extended under adjacent shops to Gordon Street. Here they played hide-and-seek among the many shelves full of wallpaper and the pattern books, which they liked to look through. A strong smell of mothballs down there is also recalled.

Bill Bottrill delighted in his job managing Sturton's, the hardware shop and ironmongers. Britons have been ironmongers since the 15th century and when John Masefield wrote of 'the dirty British coaster with the salt-caked smokestack' he said that among its cargo was 'firewood, ironware and cheap tin trays'... he could well have looked in at Bill's display at Sturton's!

CHARLES E. TATE & CO

Charles Edmund Tate was an office-boy after he left school in his native Bermondsey in south London. When WW1 broke out he was just the right age for conscription and he served his country for those years. However in France his health was affected when he was gassed to some degree, which resulted in severe respiratory problems. Back home after the war he developed tuberculosis and indeed spent some time sleeping in a tent in his garden, fresh air being considered beneficial for those suffering from TB at that time. Charles had married Lina, however, and two children, Charles Leonard and Hazel, were born during the war years before

Lina died, sadly also of TB which had been contracted from her husband. Charles moved with his children to Southend but, when they reached the age of fifteen, he suggested that they should leave home, for he had met, and later married, his second wife Marjorie who was his housekeeper's daughter. Charles was now successful in a request made to the government for a loan against his war pension. This enabled him to come to Luton and open his business at 31 Cheapside about 1933. C.E.Tate & Co became widely known as local stationers offering for sale from their small shop everything required for book-keeping (all hand-written in those days), such as account books, fountain pens, filing cabinets and loose-leaf equipment. Their own branded products

George Costen snr. with his delivery van. (EG)

were produced, which were named 'Cetco'.

In Luton Charles lived at 5 Cranleigh Gardens with Marjorie to whom a son Kenneth was born. Elder son Charles Leonard, who was Len to everyone, met his future wife Ena Taylor when they were both working at the Ekco Radio company. They were married at Southend-on-Sea. Len was not eligible for service in WW2 as he also had a problem with tuberculosis. At this time he and Ena also came to Luton to join his father in the family business, living first in St.Ethelbert's Avenue, then at 105 Cutenhoe Road and later at 262 Stockingstone Road. At home they had a family of four children, Louise, Carol, Graham and Stewart. The Cheapside shop manager at this time was George Costen whose father, Bill, was employed as van driver. His delivery duties became much greater as business expanded, and the demand for printing became such that larger premises were required for this part of the company.

Lutonian Ken Wingrove recalls C.E.Tate purchasing, in 1942, Mr. H. J. Sibley's single printing machine operation which was above the Central Garage in Stuart Street. Both he and his employer Mr Sibley moved into the newer premises at 21 King Street which became part of the growing Tate group, Len becoming a partner and controlling this area of the business. Eileen Gatward, or Miss Jeffries as she was then and who now lives in Poole, was employed at the King Street works and has good and happy memories of her time with the

Radio Coaches convey the staff outing to Brighton in 1947 (EG)

Tate's staff on the briny at Brighton, Len Tate (left), Charles Tate (right) (EG)

Tate family. There were four floors in use and Eileen, who was a shorthand typist, worked on the ground floor, except in 1947 when there were power breakdowns due to the extreme weather and the typists worked on an upper floor with blankets around them and also using overhead gas heaters. Upstairs were twenty other girls who were padding, collating, stitching and finishing the printed work. Two guillotine operators were in the basement and there was a minimum of eight machine operators. Ted Celiz, who is now in his 80s, was works manager and Ted Squires was in charge of the machinery. Other staff recalled were Mr Sibley and Les and Bernard Burgoyne. Eileen remembers how fascinating she thought it was when new printing machines were delivered, for they were far too large to be taken in through the door and upstairs to the factory floor, so upper windows were taken out and the machines hauled up on ropes. Colour printing at this time was tediously done by large letterpress machines and also only one colour at a time. During the war years the morning drink for staff who were under eighteen years old was the NAMCO chocolate supplied by the government. Staff outings were recalled with pleasure, especially those to Brighton and Southend with the usual crates of drinks being boarded as well. Eileen says that Tate's was a very friendly family firm whose directors, office and works staff worked together well.

The mid 1950s saw big changes. The printing side of the company moved out of the town centre to the Skimpot Industrial Estate and in 1959 21 King Street became the photographic suppliers Terry More Ltd. The retail stationery shop in Cheapside was sold to the manager George Costen, who advertised at that time that he had 23 years experience in the trade. He successfully continued the business here in the name of George Costen & Co. until Arndale Centre development destroyed this part of Cheapside.

Charles Tate was rather Victorian in his business approach and as such requested that his family did not visit the shop or the factory and indeed insisted that they should not bring their children and prams there. However, he achieved fulfilment and prosperity in his work and recognition and support from the people of Luton for a quarter of a century. His son Len was multi-talented and very popular. During WW2 he was known locally as a big-band musician. He was a charismatic guitarist and vocalist in Burton Gillis's Band which was resident at the George Hotel in George Street. Len was affectionately known as "Sugar" Tate and just "Sug" to his many friends and fans. He was a member of The Lansdowne Club and a Freemason. He

George Costen.

retired in 1977 and died in 1992 at the age of 80. His wife Ena, who lives in nearby Hitchin, was able to help me with this story at the age of 93. Their son Graham is still in printing and is Joint Managing Director of Tate Fastforms Ltd in Luton. Their other son Stewart also runs a print affiliated company in Milton Keynes.

TERRY MORE
Photographic/AVS

In the world of photography, 1959 was a doubly important year. It was in this year that the highly regarded company Nippon Kogaku introduced the first in a long line of internationally famous single-lens reflex cameras. The Nikon-F heralded a revolution in the development of both amateur and professional photography. In the same year, an event took place which was to become held in equally high esteem in Luton, for this is when the photographic retailers Terry More Ltd. came into being. Formed in 1959 as a joint photographic and also office equipment outlet by T. J. Olney and M. E. Birchmore, it traded from 21 King Street, the company name being an acronym formed from Terry Olney and Maurice Birchmore. This took place under the guidance of Ernest Felix, then Chairman of E. B. Lye of New Bedford Road, Luton. Edward Martin also joined the company from the outset and their collaboration was to be constant throughout the life of the company.

Terence John Olney, the prime mover behind the photographic side of the business, was born in Harrow in 1931 and came to Luton, living with his parents in Ashton Road, three years later. Secondary education was at the Luton Technical College and at this age a lifetime love of aviation was formed. After National Service with the R.A.F., Terry continued with the R.A.F. Volunteer Reserve and also, whilst holding a full pilot's licence, became Commanding Officer for the Cedars School Squadron of the Air Training Corps at Leighton Buzzard. An enthusiasm for golf developed with membership of both the Dunstable and South Beds Golf Clubs. Sadly both golf and a serious interest in aviation were somewhat curtailed when, as a young man, the distressing emergence of arthritis came into Terry's life. However, in 1955, at St. Mary's Church, he married Claire Williams who had also come to Luton at an early age when her parents moved here from Mountain Ash in the Rhondda of South Wales, when

Terry Olney and Ed Martin   (TO/EM)

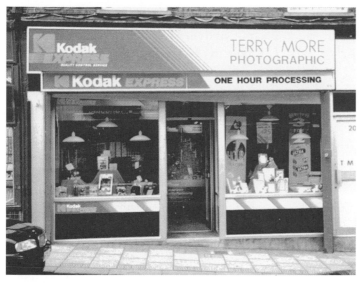

20-22 Wellington Street. (RJ)

she was one year old. Claire attended Luton High School for Girls and went on to be an established member of the Luton Girls'Choir. More recently she held the position of Chairman of BBC Radio Bedfordshire at the time of its formation and subsequently was a member of the Eastern Regional Council. They have two sons, Stephen and David. Ed Martin was born in 1941, a few miles from Luton in the village of Pegsdon. His father worked in the building industry and Ed was the youngest of eight children. At the age of 15 he went to work as an assistant to the industrial photographer at W. H. Cox in Wellington Street and it was here that he met Terry Olney who was employed in the cine department there for ten years. In 1963 Ed and local girl Patricia Ann Perrin, who came from Hexton, married in the village church. They also have two children; Debbie is a Probation Officer in Bristol and Nicholas works as a VT Post Production Co-ordinator at the BBC

Television Centre.

During the time at 21 King Street, the business expanded from its original aims to include dyeline printing for local architects, surveyors and builders, plus a wider range of expensive up-market office furniture and electronic office machinery to serve the needs of the growing industry in the town. In the mid-1960s, Terry More Ltd. was purchased outright by E.B.Lye Ltd., and the office equipment side of the business was relocated to larger premises in New Bedford Road, which left room for the expansion of the photographic business in King Street. At the beginning of the 1970s, an offer was made to the Board of E.B.Lye Ltd for the purchase of the office equipment department, which was subsequently accepted, and shortly after this disposal the Lye company also decided to dispose of 21 King Street and the business located there. At this point T.J.Olney and E.R.Martin formed a partnership to purchase the photographic business from Lye's and began trading under the name Terry More Photographic with premises leased at 78 Wellington Street, between Stuart Street and Adelaide Street. Here they specialised in sales, service and hire of audio-visual aids and allied equipment to education authorities and to industry. After several years trading here, the partnership had the opportunity of purchasing the premises, which it exercised, only to be confronted a few years later with a dwindling market for its particular expertise.

A change of direction was indicated at the beginning of the 1980s and the decision was taken to relocate the business to 49 George Street to attract more passing trade. This was quite successful, despite very stiff competition at this time. A further decision was made to purchase the photographic business of Hans Edwards in Stevenage. This again was successful, but closure was forced after two years with the unavailability of the lease on the premises, so this was integrated back into Luton. Another big decision had to be made during 1985/6 when an offer for the lease of 49 George Street was received from a big multinational company and after much deliberation, Terry More Photographic found itself back in Wellington Street, this time at numbers 20/22, formerly the haberdashery shop of Gold's, well remembered for sales of wool, buttons and cottons. After moving in, for the first week there were more opportunities for sales of these items than for photography!

The business was not long at this address before it expanded in film processing and printing with the purchase of some very expensive Gretag processing equipment from Switzerland, followed by a second unit five years later. In 1989 Vauxhall Motors Ltd. decided to outsource its entire photographic department and Terry More Photographic was well placed with its in-house facilities to offer the very competitive and convenient service which was demanded by Vauxhall Motors. This led to a further company being formed – Terry More Audio Visual Services, under the guidance of former Vauxhall employee Peter Gates. He led a very experienced team of audio-visual experts and photographers into a much wider field of conference hire, employee education, etc., both at home and around Europe. The photographic and audio-visual companies were eventually merged into one. Another independent photographer, Iain Dempster, joined the partnership in the mid 90s to head up the industrial photographic side of the business. Mention should be made of the longest serving employee. Paul Fleckney was the cheerful and knowledgeable face behind the counter and the expert film printer. Paul joined as a YTS lad and stayed until closure twenty years later.

Terry Olney and Peter Gates retired in 2000 and the final closing down, after 44 years, came about with the retirement of Ed Martin and Iain Dempster in 2003. Both Terry and Ed continue to live locally, Terry in the Bedfordshire village of Pavenham and Ed just into Hertfordshire at St. Ippollitts. It is said in the photographic trade 'If you were born before the Nikon-F, you're vintage!' Both Terry and I fit into this group and I am pleased to say that, although for something like forty years whilst I was Manager and later General Manager of University Cameras in Bute Street and Terry was busy building his own company and we were competing for the same custom, we remain good friends to this day.

S. THEODORSON

It was probably to the Shetland Islands, which were inhabited by the Picts, that the ancient Greeks and Romans gave the name Ultima Thule, 'the farthest land' or end of the World. It is here, on these bleak and hilly islands between the Atlantic Ocean and the North Sea and only 200 miles west of Norway, that our story here has its roots.

The family tree has been written back to Garth Laurenceson in 1716 and then shows the Shetlander's unusual custom of naming their sons, which includes changing even the surname in some generations. Next came Garth

Sydney Theodorson (CT)

Lawrenson, then Theodore Garthson and his son was Garth Theodoreson. He was a Greenland whaler on the good ship 'Richard'. Only in 1789 did Theodorson become the more permanent family surname. Alexander Stephen Theodorson, who was born in 1848, was a journeyman, a workman hired by the day, who had moved to Aberdeen. It was he who travelled to Luton where he married Penelope Savage. They lived at 31 Salisbury Road with their six children, Alice, Hilda, Myra, Frank, Hubert and Sydney. It is Sydney, who was born in 1893, who takes centre stage in this story. His service during WW1 was spent repairing the wooden aircraft of that time. During this period he married Prudence Hannah Brookes who was born at Edworth, near Biggleswade, and they set up home at 62 Milton Road in Luton where their sons Stanley and John were born.

Sydney ventured into many local enterprises. However, his first job in peacetime was with the Mayes brothers who were coachbuilders at 44a Stuart Street. From here he moved along to number 47, joining H. Moody as an engineer. Occasionally he worked with Dick Plater who had a business rewinding coils in Princess Street. Putting his war pension to good use, he decided to go into business on his own at 20 Stuart Street, between the junctions with Wellington Street and King Street, which is where he will be most remembered by older Lutonians. In 1925 he set up his shop as an electrical and wireless engineer on the ground floor of the old Assembly

Hall, which still stands to this day. The upper floor was used as a meeting place by the evangelistic religious movement, the Plymouth Brethren.

The first BBC broadcast from 2LO in London took place only three years earlier, and the first time there was a choice of BBC programmes on the wireless was in the same year that Sydney opened his shop. To meet the needs of the expanding market for the battery accumulator receivers, he installed a boiler at the rear of the shop which enabled the production of distilled water to be used in the accumulators which powered these new instruments, for the days of the 'cat's whisker' were gone. Of course he offered his customers the service of charging the accumulators. Also at the rear of the shop and out of the customers' sight was his workbench, which always looked quite chaotic but at which he could always lay his hands on exactly what was wanted. Business progressed well, the General Electric Company agency being held, a delivery van purchased and Theodorson's became, at the right time, a good source of almost everything electrical. The first 'Hoovers' had been imported and the Goblin Teasmade sold for £5/15/6. An Ever-Ready portable electric torch, which

Sydney's shop at the old Assembly Hall   (CT)

originally cost 12/6d, was called 'packaged electricity'. Electric fires, which today would be considered unsafe, were on sale, the luxury being able to turn them on and off at the touch of a switch. Sydney was always helpful and his knowledge in his chosen field was extensive. His son John joined him on leaving school and was later able to assist him in the shop on the busy Saturday mornings.

Sydney's widely ranging interests furthered yet more projects. In 1935 he opened a photographic studio on the side of Stuart Street which was later demolished to enable the dual-carriageway to be built. At number 109, on the corner with Rothesay Road, the public came to have their portraits taken. He employed Miss Willett to do this, for she had previously operated her own studio where she lived at 57 Wellington Street, using the name of Ada Bourne. The Theodorson studio was later moved up the road to number 18, almost next to the wireless shop, but with the Stuart Street Passage in between them. Ada worked there for about forty years. After WW2, together with five other

enthusiasts, he formed a building company which gained contracts within the construction of the new Farley Hill estate. He also shrewdly purchased and rented out other properties. In addition to this, from the age of 30, he was an apiarist, selling his bees' honey in the shop. In 1953 he was called to successfully deal with a swarm of bees which had settled on a fence in Henry Brown's timber yard. His eldest son Stan later took over the beekeeping, watching over the hives on Winsden Hill allotments. Sydney was a member of the Luton Film Society, a member of the Independent Labour Party and also keenly interested in biblical archaeology.

For exactly half a century, until 1975, this apparently insignificant little business prospered well and served the people of Luton in many ways. Sydney Theodorson never really retired, loving his job well into his 80s. The old Assembly Hall building is now gent's hairdresser's Gatsby and the old studio building next door at number 20 is now the offices of The Jaguar Drivers' Club.

 # G. A. WALLER
LIMITED

Mocked on the stage and sometimes in restaurants and the home as well, the sausage is nevertheless one of the principal dishes enjoyed by people all over the civilised world. As befits a dish borrowed from the Greeks by the Romans and probably passed on to Europe and ourselves, the sausage has survived all the mockery and remains firmly in the favour of rich and poor alike. It doesn't matter whether it comes from a grand kitchen or out of an iron pan held over a fire, it is still, without doubt, a sausage. It has defied all attempts at culinary disguise and survived every disturbing suggestion about its contents. Luton has always been fond of sausages and the town's housewives were discerning enough for many years to buy them from G.A.Waller's shops. It seems they were good judges of quality for there was no

market for a cheap sausage, the best sellers being those with a higher meat content which sold at a higher price.

The first Waller's butcher's shop opened in 1895 when George A. Waller started a little business at 52 High Town Road in Luton. He soon had more shops, opening at 27 High Street North in his home town of Dunstable in 1914, followed by three more in Luton. He first took over Mr. Poulton's butcher's shop at 57 High Town Road in 1924, then 34 Stockingstone Road on the corner with Northview Road in 1935 and 104 Dunstable Road, previously the home of Dr. John Birch on the corner with Waldeck Road, was also well-established before the commencement of WW2. Originally pork butchers, they expanded to sales of the whole range of meat of all categories. Of course all branches sold the famous Waller sausages, cold meats and pies that won many accolades. Following experiments with various seasonings their 'hand-

George Snr, George and Neil Waller   (TW)

Frank Janes and Will Cook at the opening of the Dunstable shop, c1914   (TW)

raised' pork pies won awards at Norwich, Watford and Essex Exhibitions. Finally an International Gold Medal was awarded at Olympia in 1938. They advertised "They're Wallers…you can taste the difference!"

George always lived in Dunstable, with his second wife, Sarah. They had six children, Marie, George, Elva, Neil, William and Albert, who was always known as Pete. George, the founder, died in 1938 when his two sons George and Neil took the reins of this thriving local business. George jnr. worked at High

Town Road and Neil was at Dunstable Road, with managers running the other branches. Both sons had started in the family concern as errand boys when they were about twelve years old. "We certainly worked hard," said George. "Our father insisted that we should be able to do everything. He treated us just like his other employees." In the heyday of the business there were four shops, two factories and a bakery, which was behind the Dunstable shop. Thirty-six people were employed and they even had to operate a night shift to meet demand.

Mechanisation was important and the sausage making process was organized on a production line basis. First the meat came from the cooling room on an overhead rail into the factory, where it was boned and sorted. Meat which had been selected for sausages also provided many extras for pies, black puddings, brawn etc. and the sorting took place at this stage. For sausages they wanted two-thirds lean and one-third fat which was cut up into small pieces for mincing. The powerful electric mincer was designed to run cool so that the meat was not subjected to any damaging rise in temperature. It emerged from the mincers in long streamers like spaghetti and was

placed in the bowl chopper in the exact proportions of 65% meat and 35% bread, adding seasoning containing sage, pimento, mace, coriander, nutmeg, ginger, pepper and salt with a little rusk. Next came the power filler which was a vertical cylinder with a powerful ram at the bottom and the sausage meat was forced through a nozzle at the side. Here skin of hog casing was used (or sheep casing for chipolatas) and with a little water the sausage meat emerged into the skin. This could be done at the rate of 200lbs of sausages an hour, taking only a few seconds to fill 12 feet of sausage skin, and they made two thousand pounds of sausages a week!. Twelve feet of sausage

G.A.Waller at the High Town Road shop in 1924 (TW)

James Hopgood looks on as Cyril Oliver shows how to link sausages, 1954.   (TW)

could be a little troublesome, so next they were linked. This was done by hand at a dazzling speed. The skilled craftsmen who produced these magnificent sausages gave lifetimes of service to Waller's. Many worked there for twenty years, Albert James, Frank Wood and E. Crossland for over thirty years and Cyril Oliver for more than forty years. In 1962, after fifty years, the original shop in Dunstable High Street was closed and a larger modern premises opened in the new shopping precinct, at 5 Queensway. A number of Luton businesses were

involved in this move, Johnson Fuller being the main contractors, Howards Refrigeration supplied Frigidaire equipment and Pennant Shopfitters were suppliers of stainless steel butcher's rails, hangers and shelving. A year later a well was discovered beneath the brick floor of the old shop. Roman pottery, roof tiles and arrow heads were found in it.

With government regulations making life difficult for them, in 1968 George and Neil felt that they had had enough and began to close their shops. On hearing this, one of their customers had tears in her eyes when she came into the little shop in High Town Road to buy her meat. "I shall miss coming here," she said. Some of the customers were still going to Waller's having bought their meat there when the shop had first opened. Neil said, "We shall miss all the friends we have made here more than anything else. It has been quite touching how many people have said they will miss us." In the room where millions of sausages had been

demolished and the Dunstable Road shop is now Kanzaria Optical. George, who had married Dunstable girl Queenie Hunt, first lived in Clarendon Road, then later Old Bedford Road and Halfway Avenue. In retirement in Shillington, George was a Church Warden for many years and a member of the Village Hall Committee. Neil retired to Weedon Lois in Northamptonshire.

George Waller jnr. gave a lifetime of service to local Scouting. When he was twelve he had joined the 1st Dunstable troop in 1919 and eventually became its Assistant Scoutmaster before moving to Luton and taking over the St. Matthew's troop in 1930. He was made Assistant District Commissioner in 1942 and became District Commissioner in 1948. A further promotion in 1967 was to become Deputy County Commissioner and he continued this active interest in retirement. I am sure many of us will recall him leading the singing around the huge campfire on the occasions of the scouting rallies on Popes Meadow in Luton.

George and Neil Waller at retirement, 1968   (TW)

produced, presentations were made to employees who had made and sold them over the years. The High Town shop became a ladies' and babies' outfitters for some years and is now the Royal Pharmacy. The factory behind it,which extended into Wenlock Street, is now

WALLER STUDIOS
Photography

The beginnings of this story are aligned with my own memories of something like fifty years ago. Not long after I had joined University Cameras, on the corner of Bute and Waller Streets, often among the busy Saturday morning customers would be our subject and his wife buying a 120 rollfilm ready for the job of photographing a wedding later that day. Donald Robert Wood was to advance from this to found one of the foremost photographic studios in our area.

Bob Wood was born in Croydon in 1928, the son of Irene and Robert Wood, who was a golf caddie at Addington Golf Club in Surrey. He carried for many famous names including Henry Cotton, Archie Compston and once for comedian Jimmy 'Schnozzle' Durante, but there was little money in golf in the thirties.

When war broke out, Bob, with five year old brother Brian, accompanied by minders and hundreds of other children, all labelled and carrying gasmasks and a packet of sandwiches, left Mum waving tearfully on the station platform as they set off by train for East Grinstead. Three months later Mum and the boys were reunited at 46 Third Avenue in Sundon Park, Luton. In 1942, and only 13 years old, Bob started work for haulage firm Bramhall's in Kingsway, shovelling sawdust in the sawmill at Vauxhall Motors, for transport to Scottish paper mills. His wages of £3/10/0 a week were needed at home with his father Robert in the Army. Later, Bob spent 18 months working in the REME armourer's workshop at printers Dow & Lester in Dunstable Road which like Shaw & Kilburn opposite had been requisitioned by the War Dept. Bob says they were happy days, especially the weekly test

Bob Wood (left) and Richard Cobham   (BW/RC)

firing of the repaired small arms at the quarries in Dunstable, followed by bacon sandwiches. In 1946, aged 17 years, he signed on as a regular in the Royal Artillery, finishing his service in Egypt in 1952 after transferring to the Intelligence Corps. Field security duties brought him into contact with cameras, which fired his ambition to be a professional photographer.

In 1953 Bob married Peggy Roof at St Mary's Church in Lower Sundon. Peg was born in Bow and also came to Sundon after earlier evacuation to Wales. They lived with Peg's Mum for two years while Bob worked in the press shop at Vauxhall and Peg at the Skefko Ball Bearing Company. Eventually they had sufficient capital saved for the planned enterprise. November 1955 was the important date when Bob acquired the lease on top floor offices above University Cameras. Waller Studios was born. Although at the top of two steep flights of stairs, the premises had three key advantages; they were affordable, they were central and work could be displayed at street level. The studio floor wobbled when other staff members moved above and it became routine to shout 'still!!' before making an exposure, to ensure a sharp image. However they had to rely entirely on Peg's SKF wages for over a year before any money could be taken from the business. Bob had no business training, so it was a case of learning on the job as a one- man band for the next two years, with the emphasis on the highest quality photographic work, even before profit. Established now as a

wedding and portrait photographer, Bob joined the Institute of British Photographers where he met Richard Cobham, then a photographer with the Napier Company at Luton Airport. When Richard was made redundant in 1958, he worked for English Electric at Stevenage for a short time, before joining Waller Studios. He had an impressive portfolio of industrial photographs and the ability to handle subjects on the factory floor. Bob, wishing to expand that side of the business, thought that he would be very capable of creating this position. This transpired as planned, a major breakthrough being the landing of all the Borg-Warner manual illustrations, and Bob is convinced that the standard of professional photography in Luton was upgraded from that time. He knew that success lay in high quality and invested in the best available equipment. The following year Rex Caves, who had trained with C.W.Parrott, photographers in Dunstable Road, started as a darkroom operator, going on to become an excellent photographer and valued member of the team until 1972 when he left to start his own studio in Dunstable.

In 1962 Waller Studios and Pictorial Engravers in Old Bedford Road formed between them a new company, South Midlands Lithoplates Ltd., located at 31 John Street. Offset printing, as opposed to letterpress, was seen as the future in the print industry and SML eventually became a leading supplier of offset printing plates to clients like Vauxhall Motors, White Crescent Press and

Examples of their Studio and Industrial work.   (BW)

and Richard was elected its President in 1965. Richard also received a Highly Commended Award for his photograph of a Ford Parana Sprint in the Ilford National Print Competition. Busy times indeed, but work was always interesting and often good fun, like late one Christmas Eve in the mid 60s when Richard and Bob were working in the Canaletto room in Woburn Abbey shooting the richly decorated table settings laid for the ducal family's Christmas dinner. Cut glass and priceless silver sparkled in the candlelight and reflected the soft glow of the individually lit Old Masters on the surrounding walls. Close to midnight Her Grace looked in and asked to inspect the view from the camera mounted high on its tripod. Richard and Bob will never forget the charming picture the Duchess of Bedford made in her white towelling bathrobe, perched at the top of the ladder, peering under the camera cloth at the dim upside-

Leagrave Press. Further expansion followed in 1962 with the opening of a branch studio in Pinner, Middlesex, under the direction of Roland Smith, another recruit from Parrott Studios. This year also saw Richard Cobham become a director and shareholder. Bob commenced a three-year period as secretary of the South Midlands Region of the Institute of British Photographers

down image on the screen. When the centre of Takeley in Essex was rocked by a massive gas explosion in 1962, Bob and his camera covered the event with aerial helicopter photographs for the Daily Mail. The Great Train Robbery in 1963 kept Bob and Rex busy backing up the South Beds News Agency's press coverage. Rex Caves took the first shots of the hideaway farm which the robbers used after the train hold-up. Also for the South Beds Agency, Bob scooped the national press gathered at the gates of Stoke Mandeville Hospital for the arrival of Margot Fonteyn to visit her diplomat husband Roberto Arias, crippled after a failed assassination attempt. Prior reconnaissance and early arrival secured a front page picture of Miss Fonteyn for the national press. Whitbread commissioned Waller Studios to photograph all phases of the construction of their new brewery in Oakley Road, from green field site to final completion three years later in 1969. Dozens of visits were made, taking aerial, PR and production photographs. It was extremely sad for all concerned when,

unable to agree terms with the unions, Whitbread decided to pull out altogether and close the brewery down. Bob still has a few bottles of the special opening brew! With this story we can see the Whitbread brewery, a quality example of Richard's industrial work and also a pleasing, early studio job of Bob's, when he photographed the author's two young sons in 1965.

The redevelopment of Luton town centre in the early 70s displaced Waller Studios and many other businesses, as Waller Street was destroyed in its entirety. Bob negotiated a 99-year lease from Luton Corporation to build a new purpose-built studio measuring 40 x 26ft on a plot of land in Power Court, which itself had been created by the destruction of parts of Church Street and surrounding streets and the old Fire Station. Designed as a drive-in studio for cars and large sets, this was completed in 1969 and a second building was added the following year to accommodate SML which had outgrown its premises in John Street. Frank Broomfield, David Nye and Kevin

The Power Court premises   (BW)

Calvert joined the staff at this time. Kevin is now a highly successful car photographer with several large studios in Leighton Buzzard and Spain. These were busy years at Power Court, for example during one week alone Richard, Bob and Rex were on assignments in Tenerife, in Athens and in North Wales and at the same time moving into the new premises. However as the economic problems of the 70s surfaced, (remember the three-day week and then decimalisation?), business suffered and wedding photography declined without the high street position. Bob's attempt to become more involved in the lithoplate company was thwarted by the print union's refusal to allow him to work manually in his own firm. He then decided to sell his interest in the studio to Richard Cobham, finally leaving photography in 1976. During his career Bob used many different cameras, starting with a 1951 model Kodak Retina 1a and progressing through to the accepted quality of Rolleiflex and Hasselblad, a Sinar Monorail in the studio and a Speed Graphic for the aerial jobs. Bob then spent two years delivering trucks after qualifying for his HGV licence and now he and sons Haydn and Carl own and manage the storage and distribution company Woodrush, which moved into warehouses in Pulloxhill after Bob sold his interest in SML in 1989. This company closed in 1998 and some staff took over the assets and continue business as Digital Images Ltd. now moving into Crescent Road following the sale of the Power Court premises to make way for the redevelopment of that part of the town centre. Bob described himself to me as having "Not much talent, but determination". I feel certain that both of these abilities exist in considerable strength.

Richard Cobham was born in Bridlington, the son of the Vicar of Stockton on The Forest in Yorkshire. He was educated at Stowe School and, after National Service as a Subaltern in the Northumberland Fusiliers during the Mau Mau uprising in Kenya, his first job was as a management trainee with a timber firm. His interest in photography began with the purchase of a half-plate Sanderson camera for £4/10/0. He still has this beautiful wood and brass instrument and also the photographs of birds and butterflies taken with it at that time. In 1969 he married Helen Behrens whom he had met at a party in London. Richard took Waller Studios, with colleagues Frank Broomfield, now a director, and Paul Tearle to new premises in Hitchin Road in 1986 where they laid out the 3000 sq.ft. of studio space It had a 30ft.infinity curve background and was 14ft. to the eaves. This enabled the setting of scenes from a living room to a desert and yet still be able to handle minute electronic instruments. In the new premises, demand for creative photography for advertising, display and technical manuals increased, Frank's studio skills being second to none and usefully complementing Richard's skills for location work.

Richard and Frank excelled in their colour work in the new studio, and Frank showed that he had the ability to work through endless product shots with an efficiency that was unbeatable and DIY skills that proved invaluable when creating kitchen sets when the Electrolux account was gained. Richard photographed celebrity Phil Collins in his home, for the group which manufacturerd his recording equipment. At his home in Harpenden, Eric Morecambe also posed for Richard. He particularly recalls how studio lighting has changed over his years in the profession from 500w.photoflood lamps through multiple use of flashbulbs to heavy strobe electronic flash equipment and eventually to more portable units. In its professional work Waller Studios could name both local and national companies among its customers. The list is long and includes Vauxhall Motors, Borg-Warner, Britannia Airways, Monarch Airlines, Court Line, Pasta Foods, Rodway Smith Advertising, Luton Library builders J.M.Hill & Sons, The Co-Op, H.C.Janes, Whitbread, British Oxygen, Scholl, Electrolux, Sellotape and local banks who were all on their books. In the mid 80s as engineering work began to diminish and the high-tech world arrived, their client base changed and a much greater sales effort was required to maintain a good work flow. Richard's wife Helen took on this task and played a considerable part in the continuing progress of the company. In 1998 the company was sold to Ted Downie who retained the valued name and also the staff. However, in 2000 the name of Waller Studios came down and the company was known as Visual Impact for some years, the premises are now unoccupied.

Richard and Helen have two sons, Matthew and Peter, and are retired in

Paul Tearle, Richard Cobham and Frank Broomfield at the opening of the Hitchin Road studio (RC)

Interior of the Hitchin Road studio (RC)

Harpenden. However Helen is still busy as a Justice of the Peace on the Luton Bench. As everyone has known for decades, a good photograph is worth a thousand words in impact value. Certainly industry and commerce became aware of this and also of the quality of the photographic work being executed in Luton, assisting in their commercial endeavour. They all feel privileged to have met some remarkable people, to have worked with them and are grateful to have done so. In talking to both Bob Wood and Richard Cobham again it became obvious that they have a great respect and admiration for each other. They are justly proud of the enviable reputation they held in professional photography for 45 years in the name of Waller Studios.

Top shots
in
Luton
(and in London too!)

WARWICK'S fish restaurants

There is nothing more British than fish and chips. It's one of our great institutions. However, it seems no one is sure where it originated. Charles Dickens wrote of a 'fried fish warehouse' in Oliver Twist and it was the French who invented chips (pommes de terre a la mode). The first fried fish and chip shops are thought to have been opened in Cleveland Street in London in 1860 and in Oldham in 1863 and now there are 8500 in the United Kingdom with an annual turnover of £650M. In Bradford in 1931 one shop had to employ a doorman to control the queue. The balance of protein, fibre and iron in fish and chips is an excellent source of nutrition and during WW2, Lord Woolton, the Minister of Food, decided that fish and chips should be among the few foods not to be rationed.

In Luton we were fortunate for almost fifty years to have great local fried fish and chips shops and restaurants bearing the name Warwick. Frederick George Warwick lived in Brook Street, Luton in the 1920s, working in the building industry, but he could see a downturn in trade and started Warwick's Ltd. by buying and leasing properties selling fish and game. By the time he had moved to St.Albans and become Mayor in 1933, Warwick's Ltd. had shops in Luton, Harpenden, Dunstable, Watford, Fleetville and St. Albans, which branch also sold game. He had two sons, Maurice born in 1903 who attended St.Albans School when they lived in the town, and Denis born in 1910 who went to St. Gregory's School in Downs Road, Luton, when they later lived in Luton again. Both his sons ran the business, with Maurice concentrating on the 'fried fish' and Denis on the 'wet fish'.

Warwick's had three shops in Luton. Numbers 12-14 High Town Road between The Bricklayer's Arms and The Railway Tavern, 87 Chapel Street was on the corner with Ebeneezer Street and 41 Park Street

12-14 HighTown Road (RJ)

was on the corner with St. Ann's Lane. Known as Warwick's Fish Restaurants, some offered the extra pleasure of supper rooms where, instead of eating from newspaper as you walked along the street, you could feel quite a 'toff' and eat your meal at a table. During WW2 fish was in great demand as it was not rationed and Luton's fish came through a regional system from Fleetwood, although a Hitchin wholesaler distributed fish supplies from Grimsby. Later on, Maurice's son Alban came into the business and recalls an era of total trust where the agents at the major ports, such as Hull and Grimsby, would send telegraph messages, (which were delivered by boys on bicycles!), or telephone in the morning. Alban would buy the fish based on the agent's word. This would be delivered by train at 6am the following morning, with payment at the end of the week and not a computer print-out or accountant to be seen! During the 1950s two Warwick shops

Denis Warwick completes the London to Brighton VCC run in 1983   (MW)

were closed, but the Park Street premises continued trading successfully, providing our favourite food for two more decades, eventually closing in 1973. Joan Warwick, wife of Denis, remembers that all the staff in the shops used to talk 'backslang'. This was a popular way of talking amongst themselves so that customers would not know what was being said. For example, 'two and six' would become 'owt an exis'. The Park Street site is now the Dixy Chicken and Pizza Takeaway.

Denis Warwick had many outside

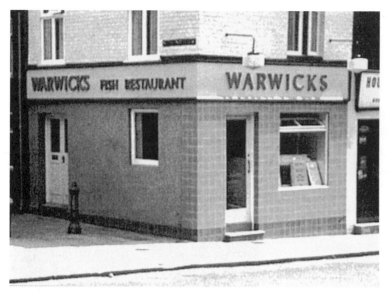

41 Park Street   (AS)

taken of his family were recently shown on television during the Anglia Television series "The Way We Were". The producer of these programmes tells me that "one of the series highlights for me was undoubtedly the films made by Denis Warwick". I am grateful to her for supplying the still of the Park Street shop which was taken from one of those films.

interests, including rally driving. With his brother Maurice he entered the Monte Carlo Rally three times in the late 40s and early 50s using a Mk V Jaguar and an Austin A-90. Maurice's son Alban shared the driving when he was 17 and became the youngest driver in the Rally. The brothers also competed in the R.A.C. Lisbon and Daily Express Round Britain Rallies. When Denis retired from rally driving, he bought a 1904 Humber and made forty consecutive runs on the Veteran Car Club London to Brighton Rally. A qualifying run is when the car arrives in Brighton before a set time. Cinematography was another hobby, and such was his enthusiasm and ability in this field that the 9.5mm and 16mm films

Fried fish and chips have never been more fashionable. You can eat them at The London Dorchester hotel, on a South African cliff top, in the desert of Oman, whilst gambling in the Las Vegas casinos and even in China where they are served with sugar! Nowadays a quarter of the white fish consumed in the UK and 10% of all potatoes are sold through fish and chip outlets. These have many amusing names such as The Chip Inn, The Jolly Friar, The Perfect Plaice and The Cod Father. But we give thanks to the Warwick family for just giving our local shops their own name and willing us the very happy memories of their superior culinary delights which were in our town for so long … Long live the Fried Fish and Chip Shop!

J. Webdale & Sons, Ltd.

The Luton Union Central Workhouse in Dunstable Road was completed in 1836. At this time young John Webdale was a hairdresser at 38 George Street and also served on the old Board of Health. He had come from a farming family and it is known that he used to keep pigs in a field next to his business in George Street. In February 1838 he decided, whilst also keeping an eye to business, to help some of those less fortunate than himself who were residing therein. He agreed "to learn one or two of the boys in the workhouse to Shave, Cut Hair and Set Razors for the sum of £3 each". The Workhouse Board agreed to this, but each pauper boy being apprenticed was required to have a Health Certificate signed by the Surgeon, stating that he was sound and healthy and fit to be put out to apprenticeship.

In 1841 John Webdale removed his business into one of the first buildings erected in Wellington Street, then still open fields, and began trading in hardware. He was believed to have built only the second shop there and the cost to Mr Webdale for this site was £80. He moved from George Street and lived there. Later additional purchases extended the property through to King Street, and warehouses and annexes were built to accommodate the ever-increasing business. In the following years, when separate wholesale and retail businesses

John Webdale as Luton's 6th Mayor

developed simultaneously, The House of Webdale became well-known to everyone throughout the town and neighbourhood.

In 1881 John Webdale, who was living at 9 Studley Road, became the sixth inhabitant to hold the office of Mayor of the Borough of Luton and he had also been a Director of the Luton General Cemetery Company in 1854. He was assisted in the management of his company by his son, who was also John and who in his turn served his native town for a long period as Councillor and Alderman. In 1912 their business of

Hardware & General Factors and Grocers' Sundriesmen became a private limited company, J. Webdale & Sons Ltd. The management passed to John Henry Snell Webdale, grandson of the founder, who also lived in Studley Road, at number 29, his brother Frederick Charles of Westbourne Road being associated with him. Fred managed the furniture department and one of his daughters worked in the accounts office. Another daughter worked with Mr Cox in his nearby art shop. John Henry, who was always known as Harry, gave 24 years service to Bedfordshire County Council, seven of them as an Alderman when he filled the vacancy caused by the retirement of Alderman G. Wistow Walker. He was also thirty years a director and fifteen years Chairman of Luton Building Society, Treasurer and Life Deacon of Bury Park Congregational Church and one of the oldest members of Luton Bowling Club. Joan Greenacre,

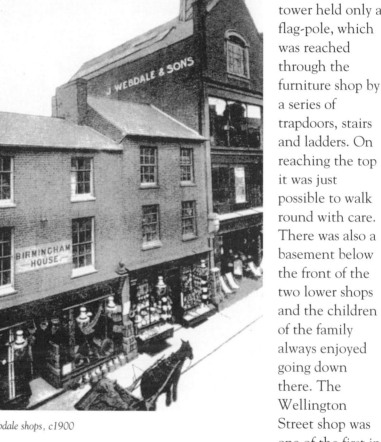

The Webdale shops, c1900

who lives in Northamptonshire and is the grand-daughter of John Henry, recalls being told that the Webdale building was the tallest in the town until the Town Hall was built; it certainly afforded a good view from the tower which is still visible. The tower held only a flag-pole, which was reached through the furniture shop by a series of trapdoors, stairs and ladders. On reaching the top it was just possible to walk round with care. There was also a basement below the front of the two lower shops and the children of the family always enjoyed going down there. The Wellington Street shop was one of the first in the town to have a telephone installed, you just asked for Luton 41.

I remember going to Webdale's as a child, accompanying my father on early-closing afternoon when he would purchase wholesale stock for resale in his general store in Leagrave. Webdale's were specialists in domestic hardware and

Webdale's bold advertising on one of Luton's first trams on their first day in 1908

equipment, china and glass, house furnishings, upholstery, and they were also bedding makers. Their store was crammed from floor to ceiling with hardware of every description. A full list would take many pages but it is worth recalling some of the items which nowadays are often seen only at antique and collectors' fairs. Hardware included mincers and graters, cut tacks and brads, wringers and stands, heating stoves, shovels and tongs and coal hods. The Brooms & Brushes Dept. stocked sisal, jute and cotton twine, blind cord and jug mops. Within Woodware were scullery mats, clothes horses and meat safes. The Paper/Stationery section sold cheese paper, ink and gum, doyleys and bags of all kinds. On the China & Glass shelves were hot water bottles, fruit preserving jars and lamp chimneys. For the gardener there was an enormous selection from canes and raffia to roofing and garden rollers and the four-tine warranted English made digging fork cost 3/6d (17 1/2p). Grocers' Sundries was a separate department which offered starch, candles and night lights, patent medicines, cough cures, pudding powders, flakes and scourers, size and glue and

The Webdale shops, c1920

Reckitt's specialities. They advertised that they offered French polishing, bedding purified and remade, blinds and cornice poles fitted and that upholstery of every description was 'done on the premises by expert workmen'. Another interesting advertisement was headed "A Grate Success" and suggested that Namo Liquid Black would make your grate look like polished ebony. It dried hard, resisted heat, lasted for months and saved daily blackleading. It cost 1/- (5p) a bottle, including the brush. Add to all this rugs and linoleum, travelling trunks, fires, kettles, razor sets, wood dyes, mending wool and press studs and you will just begin to appreciate what an Aladdin's cave of wonder Webdale's was.

Between the wars some modernisation was carried out to the frontages of the shops and also the china department and the offices. During this work it was discovered that for a long time in his office John Henry

had been sitting over a deep well, albeit an empty one. It was promptly filled in. At the end of WW2 a change of policy was decided upon, a decision brought about by a variety of causes, but mostly due to the increasing age of the directors. British Home Stores had made an offer for the rear part of the premises including the loading bay and the King Street entrance. They were anxious to own this entrance enabling their vehicles to reach the rear of the store. This was agreed and in March 1947 Webdale's became solely wholesale. The property in King Street and Wellington Street which occupied numbers 21 to 27, was disposed of and the business was transferred to Products House at 46A Alma Street where a modern warehouse was built. The new premises afforded every facility for handling and distributing the goods required by shopkeepers of the town and district. John Henry Webdale became Governing Director whilst the Managing Director was his son John Alexander who lived in Kensworth and who was always known as Alec. He had been President of the Old Dunstablians and met Mr. Khwaja Nazimuddin, Prime Minister of Pakistan, when he paid a return visit to the Grammar School where they had both been pupils. He was a keen British Legion man, Superintendent of the Bury Park Sunday School and during WW2 he was Divisional Commandant 'E' Division, Beds Special Constabulary. His great love was cricket and he played for the Luton Town 2nd XI for many years. As factors recognized on the approved lists of most Manufacturers' Associations, Webdale's were in a position to buy in the best markets and to offer goods at highly competitive prices and their motor vans made regular and frequent deliveries within a 25 miles radius of Luton. Coincidentally, the Governing Director had been born at 46 Alma Street, adjoining the new premises. This was also the property of the firm, it having been built by his father on his marriage in 1867.

Numbers 21 to 27 Wellington Street have seen many new businesses in later years. Ashley Russell, John Edwards and Easiphit Fine Shoes among others followed the departure of Webdale's and currently 21 is The XXX Zone, 23 is Ramstad, 25 is First Call and 27 is the Espresso Internet Café. Their space in Alma Street, which was acquired by Home Counties Newspapers and used for photo-engraving, is now the Bedfordshire & Luton Community NHS Trust car park.

In 1948, the company had recorded that it had seen the town grow from a population of under 6,000 inhabitants to over 110,000 at that time. The reputation built up during the passage of these years was one of which they were justifiably proud. The motto of the founder stayed with them through all of their more than a century in Luton, it was 'Service, Quality and Value'. In fact they had been serving Luton for 113 years when the company closed in September 1954. It was the second family concern to close in Luton within two months, Hannibal Bonds having closed in July. John Blythin, President of the Luton Chamber of Trade, said "It is rather a pity to see the older family firms cease to function and their place taken by multiples, but it is a sign of the times". In a letter announcing the closure John Alexander Webdale wrote "I can assure you that the decision to abandon this business in favour of farming, a lifelong interest, has not been taken lightly". A few weeks later his father John Henry died at the age of 82.

H.WHITE

One very warm July afternoon it was pleasing to drive around the Norfolk coast to the fishing port and seaside resort of Wells-Next-The-Sea. Here it was enjoyable to once again meet Barbara and Jack White, who were both 92, and to sit reminiscing in their conservatory, followed by tea and cakes in their sunny garden. It had been possibly forty years since we last met them but then we had been their customers, receiving excellent and knowledgeable service in the purchase of the correct footwear for our young sons. I am sure many of you reading this will have also visited their Luton shop at 65 Wellington Street.

White's boot and shoe shops began life many years earlier with George White who was born in Bromham, three miles north of Bedford, in the first half of the nineteenth century. His father had been a carter carrying goods between Bromham and Bedford. It was George who came to Luton in 1860 and went into business making and selling boots and shoes at 12 Park Street West. With his wife they had four children, but it was his son Harry, born in 1865, who was to progress the business into one of those most well-remembered in Luton.

Dunstable girl Minnie Millicent Mead, who had been dating Harry's brother Frank, was very surprised one Sunday to hear her wedding banns being read out in church. Surprised because it was not Frank to whom she was being betrothed, but to his brother Harry who had arranged for them to be read without her knowledge! The marriage did go ahead, however, and they set up home at No.2 Gordon Street (currently the British Pregnancy Advisory Service), moving later to Cromwell Road

Minnie and Harry White (JW)

176

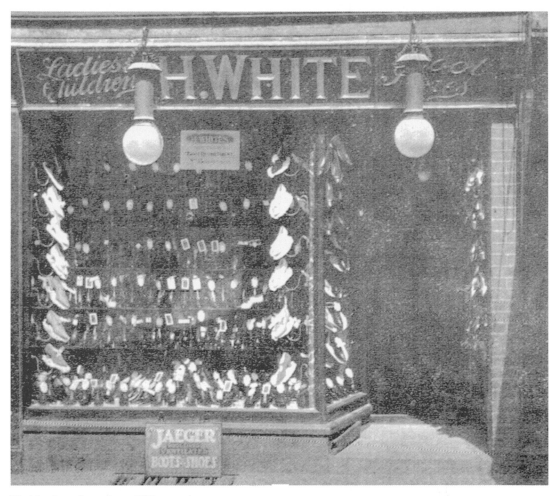

The Manchester Street shop   (JW)

and finally to 6 Alexandra Avenue. They had ten children, some of whom worked in the expanding family business. Victor, Mabel and her husband Ted Adams and the youngest son Frank John (always known as Jack) worked with their father. Near to their home, Manchester Street was the scene for their empire where for many years five shops bore the respected name of H. White above their displays of boots and shoes. Numbers 24 and 26 held the stocks of ladies' shoes, number 28 was for the children and number 30 was where the men of the town called. Jaeger, Lotus and Delta agencies were held when in 1925 prices ranged between 16/6 (82p) and 45/- (£2.25). At that time they advertised "Thousands of people suffer minor or major discomfort because their feet fall between the standard sizes of shoes. The proper course is to go to H. White's. There with due regard to price, style and serviceability at its very highest they will find a Shoe

Comfort they have never known before. *They will get a Shoe that fits!"* In the following year they suggested that you "Wend Your Way in White's Shoes".

On the opposite side of Manchester Street, number 35 held stocks of leggings and farmers' boots and was also the Repair Department. Three men worked on repairs, stitching and finishing in the workshop where Harry always installed the latest machines, including a Victor machine which stitched through the welt and a Blake Sewer which sewed through the inner sole. Bespoke boots and shoes were commonplace at this time, there being two upstairs rooms on the premises which were full of customers' personal lasts, although measurements were always taken before production just in case the feet had changed in some way. Cork insertions and thicker cork soles were often required for those whose legs were not of the same length, enabling them to walk more easily. Removals expert W. J. Edwards, often known as Billy or affectionately as Hoppy, who became Luton's Mayor in 1947, was a valued customer who required this service. The first x-ray machine to assist in shoe fitting outside of London was installed in Manchester Street and gave a top view and a second side view of a customer's feet which was helpful in providing arch support. It eventually became a nuisance, with children constantly wanting to see their toe bones wriggling, and many Monday mornings would see Luton Town F.C. trainer Billy Lawson bring an injured player in with a request to use their x-ray machine. The White family believed

that half of Luton were their customers! Number 35 had closed at the end of WW1 but the remaining White's shoe shops continued in Manchester Street, through WW2, until 1956. Harry, who retired at the age of 55, had often lectured at the Union Chapel in Castle Street. He died in 1950, aged 85, his wife Minnie having predeceased him by five years.

The youngest son Jack, who was educated at Dunstable Grammar School, boarding from the age of 7, joined the men's department in 1926 at the age of 15. Being very much the youngest of the family it was something of a shock at the age of 45 to find that Victor and Ted were ready to retire. The company was then sold to shoe retailers Norvic Footfitters Ltd., who retained the valued name of White on the shops and remained there until demolition of this side of Manchester Street took place. They were all demolished to make way for St. George's Square.

At St. Andrew's Church in 1941 Jack had married Barbara Hawkins of Avondale Road where she had been bombed-out during a wartime air-raid. They had met at the Luton Lawn Tennis & Bowling Club and after the war set up home in Wychwood Avenue. With the closure of the company and with many years of shoe retailing experience behind him, together with Barbara he searched for new premises in which to continue their career. Eventually they noticed herbalist C.P.Clegg's disordered shop at 65 Wellington Street where a very small notice of about 4" in size stated "these premises for sale". A deal was made with

Barbara and Jack White in 2002.

grey carpet containing bold alphabet motifs, was always busy with sales of Start-rite shoes from Southall of Norwich and Clark's shoes from C & J Clark. Every child was measured and C,D,E and even F fittings were kept in stock when no-one else in town did so. On opening they had advertised that "the most important thing that goes into Start-rite shoes are your children's feet!"

Barbara's brother Roland took over the Wellington Street shop when Jack and Barbara retired in November 1969, and remained there until 1984. It now houses the ladies' hairdressers, "Nutters". Roland still lives in Knoll Rise in Luton. At the age of 92 Jack White gave up bowling, but he and Barbara continued to enjoy their retirement in colourful Wells-Next-The-Sea. Sadly Barbara died in 2004.

Mr Clegg and in August 1956, F.J.White, children's footwear specialist, was born. Everyone told them that they would never make a living up there beyond Stuart Street where mothers would find it difficult to take their children across the busy road. However, their expertise proved very successful, there even being a queue of customers on the opening day! Their shop, with the memorable gold and

White & Hall Ltd.

It was a sight for sore eyes to have Vicky Stone call one sunny afternoon. I had an eye to get her father's story for this book, we quickly saw eye to eye. Now I'm up to my eyes in writing it! … surely you've guessed that this is all about an ophthalmic optician, a person who makes and sells optical instruments, especially spectacles, and is skilled in optics.

Victor Clarence Hall is our subject. Born in Folkestone in 1915 he was the third child born to master builder Arthur George Hall and his wife Florence Louise.

Victor Hall (VSt)

Victor attended the Harvey School in Folkestone and became interested in optics in school, having excelled in the sciences, with a special interest in photography. From school he worked at a chemist's in Folkestone where the pharmacist suggested that he had a flair for optics. In 1936 he was granted a diploma in visual optics and sight testing together with Fellowship of The Worshipful Company of Spectacle Makers. He was also a Freeman of the City of London. In 1939 he married Anne Maxfield and also joined opticians Savory & Moore who traded as Power & Son in Walton on Thames, where they set up home.

World War 2 was to make a break in his career when he became an instrument maker in the R.E.M.E. He rose through the ranks to become Captain and was known to all as Henry (remember Henry Hall?). He served in the North African Campaign through El Alamein and Sicily where it was his responsibility to keep the service vehicles on the road. He was proud to say that he was a Desert Rat and to wear the Africa Star. During this time in Walton On Thames, Anne had given birth to Dawn, and Vicky was born later in 1946.

With the war behind him Vic was looking for advancement in his profession and in 1946 saw a suitable advertisement in their trade magazine "The Opthalmic Optician", which was especially suitable as it also offered accommodation. It was Duberly & White who traded in pharmacy and optics at their shop at 27 Cheapside in Luton who were advertising. They were looking for someone to assist Walter White in sight testing in Cheapside whilst Walter worked from the Market Hill shop. George Duberly was the chemist in the partnership. They also traded at various times as chemists on Market Hill, in Bishopscote Road, in High Town Road, in Park Street, George Street and as Reid's Chemists in Dunstable Road. The Cheapside building had been occupied by tailors, Carrington & Son, at the turn of the century and had other uses before Duberly & White were in residence. Victor was successful in gaining the position with them and moved to Luton, settling in above the shop with his family. They quickly made friends with Sidney and Hilda Manning, the newsagents at number 23.

Duberly & White, who advertised 'Sight is essential to success', progressed well but Vic was amused to find that the people of Luton called the firm "Jubilee & White", or perhaps it was just the Lutonian accent! The Labour Government elected after the war had introduced the National Health Service and by 1950 both eye tests and most spectacles were available without charge. People who had not previously worn glasses suddenly visited opticians to have their sight tested free. Opticians, and locally Vic in particular, were kept very busy indeed. In 1956 Vic's name 'went up in lights' when he became Managing Director, and the company name changed to White & Hall for the rest of its years serving the residents of Luton and the full name was retained on the shop fascia after Walter White's retirement. Vic's wife Anne had her part in the business, for she was receptionist and also received those with hearing problems when the Bonochord Hearing Centre was introduced into the Cheapside shop. She often laughed when recalling an incident at reception one day. A rather prim lady sat down in front of her, looked sternly into her face and said "Now I understand that for an eyesight test I will need to go into a darkened room with a man, can you assure me that this will be alright?" Anne as receptionist replied "Yes madam it will be alright, he's my husband!" Following his wartime experiences, Vic was very much anti-German, which one day resulted in him throwing out the representative of the Zeiss Company who had called to sell him some of their German spectacle frames. Vicky recalls, one evening whilst doing her homework in the shop, telling her father that her teacher's handwriting was so bad that she couldn't read it. To her father it appeared good handwriting, so Vicky was quickly ushered in for a sight test which showed her to be very short-sighted. Vic had a broad taste in music and loved his hi-fi centre, often playing stereo records in Cheapside that would have the public standing outside listening. At Coronation time he made his own television set. He was also an enthusiastic Freemason.

Compulsory purchases to enable the Arndale Centre to rise brought 27 Cheapside, together with many other buildings, into demolition. So in 1967 the Hall family moved to 108 New Bedford Road, on the corner with Cromwell Hill, which had been built on the land formerly used as his stables by brewer J.W.Green. The business continued by moving it in 1968 to 46 New Bedford Road, which had previously been occupied by travel agents Seamarks Bros. This was leased from Mrs Bone of the nearby musical instrument shop. It prospered here under Victor Hall's qualified and competent guidance for a further eleven years. Vic retired in 1979, all company records being purchased by local opticians P.G.Allder. In retirement he enthusiastically grew fuschias. Number 46 is now occupied by Luton Army & Navy Stores. Vic died in 1996, aged 81, his wife Anne having predeceased him by five years, aged 75. Daughter Vicky, in retirement still lives locally in the village of Tebworth, having previously spent 25 years with Marks & Spencer in their George Street, Luton, Customer Service Department.

The earliest authentic reference to spectacles dates from 1289 when Sandro di Popozo wrote "I am so debilitated by age that without the glasses known as spectacles, I would no longer be able to read or write. These have recently been invented for the benefit of poor old people whose sight has become weak"... It could be me! ... I'm very pleased I consulted Victor Hall many years ago!

Sight Testing  **Spectacle Repairs**

Steward of the Manor and Clerk to the Justices, William Austin was Luton's most distinguished historian, but during his lifetime another of the same name was born only a few miles away close to the Green in Caddington. This William Austin arrived in 1893, one of twelve children born to his mother and farmworker father.

After schooling William joined the army for the duration of WW1 and in 1918 at All Saints Church in Caddington married Mabel Grace Burgess from Slip End, who was also from a very large family. William worked in a Luton hat factory and they lived at 48 High Town Road where two of their children, Irene and Douglas, were born. In 1918 he began his first commercial enterprise at the Luton Town Football Club ground, into which he pushed a green covered wagon from which he sold sandwiches, pies and cups of tea to the club supporters. This was the beginning of a successful career feeding the people of Luton!

William Austin (MC)

A baker's shop was opened in High Town Road and also at 35 Wellington Street, with a bakehouse in the basement producing their bread and cakes, their son Douglas being the baker. The White Rose Catering Company had arrived. The present descendents in the family believe the name came from William's love of gardening, for by now the family had moved out of Luton to a house in Lower Woodside with an orchard which held at least 200 fruit and hazelnut trees. Down the garden the original covered wagon from the football ground was now relegated to being the chicken house! Their new house was named Rosemount and their daughter Mavis was born here. During WW2 the Home Guard meetings were held here, with training taking place in the orchard. Business prospered, with cafes at 81 Church Street, 32 Park Street, 111 Guildford Street, 7 Peel Street and at 16 Leagrave Road in the Bury Park area, also a portable one in Windmill Road serving the workers from

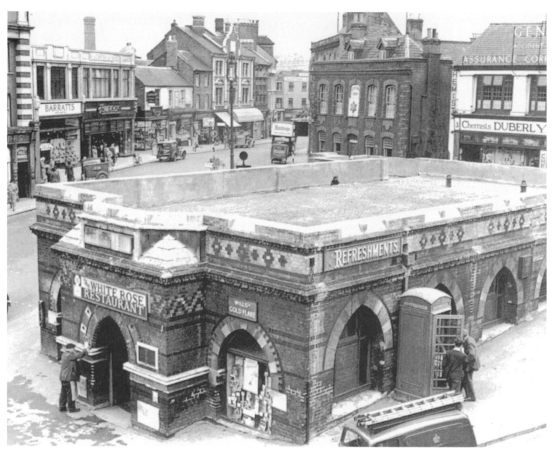

The Restaurant in the Corn Exchange building

the Vauxhall factory. The baker's shop at 35 Wellington Street became the registered office. A stall was also taken when the open market was held on Park Square. It was very much a family concern, with Aunt Beat and Uncle George in Park Street, Aunt Nell in Guildford Street, Aunt Doll in Mill Street and Bill and May, as they were usually known, at the most successful outlet and that most remembered by Lutonians which occupied the ground floor of the 1869 Corn Exchange in George Street. Before this historic building took shape corn was bought and

sold on Market Hill. Then the old Market House was demolished before the Corn Exchange was begun. When completed it was used as a meat market on Saturdays and a plait market on Mondays besides being the trading centre for farmers and corn dealers. The old Court Leet was held there and the 'Statty Fair' was held about its walls until 1929. In the hands of White Rose Catering the upper floor was hired out for wedding functions and as a dance hall, and it was from here that May controlled the office organising the outside catering for children's parties and the weddings. Here, as you entered on the ground floor, to your left was the workmen's bar where you could buy a good cup of tea and a 'wad', slang at that time for a sandwich, cake or bun. To the right was the tea shop offering more dainty sandwiches and cakes from waitresses, dressed in smart white pinafore aprons and head bands, who would serve you at your table with tea services bearing the White Rose crest. Millie was the manageress and Rose and Alice were the cooks. All types of meals were available here and at the cafes. Roast beef or pork meals with vegetables were costing 2/6 and an extra 6d for your pudding, or you could always have a fry-up. Cakes were all of twopence or threepence and sixpence bought you a jug of tea. Stan Clark, who worked across the road in Fisher's the butchers, recalls buying a jug of tea and selling it to his colleagues back in the shop at threepence a cup, making himself a small profit. He also remembers that an unseen gentle lift of the pinball machine usually produced the hoped-for win and the desired prize of the Woodbine cigarette. During WW2 The White Rose in George Street was a favourite with the American GIs stationed locally, often forming queues outside. Mrs. Grace Goring ran the forces canteen here for six years when boys and girls in uniform could always get a cup of tea or coffee, a pork pie or a Chelsea bun. It closed in March 1946, when it was estimated that more than two million cups of tea had been served to allied services from all parts of the World.

This was a flourishing and rewarding business which began to slow down in the 1950s, and the George Street premises finally closed in 1953 when the lease was not made available for renewal. The building which had been variously described as 'a noble edifice' and 'a dunces cap' had begun to present problems in 1951 when the council warned that the roof was unsafe, that rafters had rotted and that four of the five main trusses were crumbling. Taxi drivers who parked outside the building were advised to park elsewhere. In this year the clock tower and upper story were removed. In spite of the experts' reports however, William Austin scoffed at the idea of it being dangerous, saying 'I wish they would leave it as it is for another fifty years. If I lived it out I would stay.' Final demolition took place in April 1953 and gardens were laid out in time for the Coronation celebrations. Later the underground toilets were demolished and it is now an open seating area. William Austin was involved in Caddington life, playing cricket and football, serving on Caddington Council and also as a Church Warden at All Saints Church for 35 years. He died in 1972.

WOOTTON & WEBB, Ltd.
Chemists & Opticians

Before the introduction of the National Heath Service in 1948, doctors used to charge for seeing patients. It actually started in 1912 but then was only for those earning less than £5 which meant that many poor people would depend on the chemist for advice. This most certainly was the case with our subject here, for they were chemists to the growing population of Luton for more than a century. Peter Wootton is known to have been a 'chymist' in Park Street in 1839; fourteen years after that he had moved into Market Place as a 'Chemist/ Druggist, dealer in British wines and retailer of stamps'. A further fourteen years later his son had joined him in the business and the name of Peter Wootton now appears in a Bedfordshire List of Gentry. At the turn of the century he has an associate, John Henry Webb, and so the respected name of Wootton & Webb appeared at number 20 George Street. This was between the narrow passageway which led into the covered market and the historic public house, The Plough, which was built in 1833. I am sure the magnificent, extraordinary interior of the shop and the 'medical smell' which always greeted you on entry, will be remembered by many of us.

The greater part of this story concerns the memories of one person who worked at Wootton & Webb for ten years, joining them when she was just 15. Theresa Keilty had come south to Luton with her parents from County Durham and was learning office skills at Berridge's Commercial School in Dunstable Road and finding that office work was not really for her. One day, when shopping in Wootton & Webbs, she was so impressed with the place that she surprised herself, for she says that she was a shy girl, by asking if she could work there. After an on-the-spot brief interview, she had the job and then had to break the news to her father that she was not continuing

20 George Street

with the shorthand and typing classes. This was in 1944 when Mr. Frederick Webb was in charge of the shop, together with his sister Evelyn who was a member of the Wesleyan Methodist Chapel in Waller Street and also supported many local charities. Mr. George Shelton, who was the optician, lived in London Road and was an enthusiast for and could speak Esperanto, an international language which had been published in 1887. Other staff recalled from this time are Pam Sharpe, Vera Woodward, Lois Slater, also Bessy Misseldine and John Angwin who were the dispensers. Theresa recalls that Miss Evelyn Webb's working rules were quite strict, for she was not allowed to wear ear-rings or to use any nail polish. She was also at first very surprised at the size of the premises which appeared quite narrow from the street. They had been extended back into what was once the garden at the rear of a house and she says "It was huge!" On the ground floor, in addition to that which was visible to the public, there was the optical workroom, the dispensary and then narrow stone stairs which led down into the basement storeroom. The building extended the full length of the public passageway right up to the market entrance and indeed beneath it. Theresa always took the basement steps very tentatively, shielding her eyes as well, for once in the basement she was often accompanied by rats. Two windows on the market passageway were used for the display of cameras and the promotion of amateur photography, 'the fashionable pastime' as Kodak called it. In the 1920s sales of sensitized glass plates and printing-out papers were on the increase. Four small stalls in the passageway were also built onto the outside of this wall which were rented by market traders who made their weekly payments to Wootton & Webb at the end of Saturday trading. The first floor of the building was as large as the ground floor and housed the optical department, another storeroom, the darkroom where customers' enlargements were made and also the busy Wholesale Department which, by van, supplied other chemists throughout the local area.

Theresa's first job was to dust the many one-pound packets of cotton wool which were stored in the shop, just below the ceiling. The walls were covered with fine mahogany display cabinets and 'hundreds of wooden drawers', all with cards bearing euphonious Latin names which were dropped into brass holders on the front of each drawer. There was a till and an upright telephone with a cradle at the side on which hung the earpiece. To the rear of the shop were large drums containing metol and hypo for the processing of customers' films for, even then, at Wootton & Webbs your films were developed and printed on the premises. There were shelves full of glass jars containing all the requirements for their personal medicines which were prepared using pestle and mortar, for to help their customers they often mixed their own patent cures for common illnesses. Linaments were prescribed and poultices and inhalants and flu reliefs and tonics. Elderly people would call for help

Interior of 20 George Street

with their waterworks or constipation problems. These were all recorded in the prescription book so that, if a satisfied and possibly partly cured customer returned asking for more, the details were ready to hand. For private paying customers, these prescriptions were always wrapped in brown paper and sealed with wax, the lit Bunsen burner always being ready for this purpose. Sometimes enquiries were made about customers' pets when the same remedies given to clients could be prescribed, but in smaller doses. Staff also had to be observant and notice if a customer had altered a doctor's prescription to obtain more medication than was known to be

correct. Theresa recalls selling Beecham's Powders, which in their earlier form as Pills were described as 'the gentle reliable and effective laxative, worth a guinea a box'. Also Carter's Little Liver Pills, Bile Beans, Andrew's Liver Salts, Vick Vaporub, LiquaFruta, Virol and Woodward's Gripe Water. She used to sell twenty-five Aspirins for 6d, which they said 'could be taken in train, tram, the house or anywhere!', and strips of five Aspro for 5d. Another job was helping make up the shop's own brand of talcum powder and bath salts, all boxed and ribboned for 3d. When word got around that Brylcreem or Yardley's cosmetics had come in, queues would form outside the shop. In her days behind the counter, contraceptives were not on display as they are now, but kept out of sight in one of the lower wooden drawers, and male customers for these would nervously first enquire from her if there was a gentleman serving.

Wootton & Webb were also opticians offering sight testing, eye examinations and optical repairs. They suggested in their 1918 advertisement that people ask themselves 'Do I Need Spectacles?' and then 'IF it is necessary to remove small print or small objects to a distance of more than twelve or fourteen inches from the eye to obtain clear vision…IF vision is clear for a moment, then suddenly becomes confused or blurred…IF when reading, the eyes tire so that it is necessary to close them and rest for a time before resuming…IF headache and neuralgia occur frequently…YOU DO'. They later stated that their opticians had 'All that science can give, All that artistry can add'. In addition to the constant medical aroma, a less pleasant odour came from the sheep dip which was produced and sold to local farmers. Another of Theresa's jobs was to carry the day's takings in the leather bag provided across the road to the National Westminster Bank and place it in the nightsafe. On one of these journeys, the bag became unlocked and rolls of notes fell out onto George Street. Luckily the taxi drivers parked outside quickly came

to her rescue. Mrs. Chambers from the George Street jewellers was a customer as was Lady Keens who often bought gifts of chocolate truffles in for the staff. Another memory, from late opening duties, is of the Salvation Army brass band playing in front of the Corn Exchange on Sunday evenings.

In 1952, at St. Joseph's Church, Theresa married Lutonian and master blockmaker in the hat trade, Mark Robbins and they are still Luton residents. In 1954 Evelyn Webb made the surprise decision to close the business. Wootton & Webb had looked after, cared for, healed and maybe even cured the people of Luton for over a hundred years. It was possibly the most respected chemist's shop in town despite there being others, indeed Duberly & White and Boots were close to them on the adjacent sides of the Corn Exchange. The valuable prescription book was sold to Martin's, the chemists, and the processing drums were purchased by local photographer C.W.Parrott. Theresa says 'when those drums were removed it was like Hamelin!…there were mice everywhere!' She was able to continue working with Co-Op Chemists, but says of her time with Wootton & Webb, 'I loved every minute'. The clothiers, Milletts, moved into number 20, removing the graceful Georgian bay windows. It is now part of the Debenhams store.

SUBSCRIBERS

Elvira & Brian Adams
David Alexander
John Alexander
John C. Allen (Allen's Taxis)
Anne Allsopp
Mr. & Mrs. John Arnold
Mrs. A. Baldwin
Mr. A. J. Barringer
Peter Bebb
Patricia Boxford
Mrs. M. E. Brooks
Rowan Brown
Roy & Hilary Brown
Elsie Buck
Paul & Jean Bullimore (née Clemitson)
Sylvia E. Cale
Philip Chapman
Mrs. B. C. Clark
Mr. & Mrs. S. Clark
Tony & Sheila Clitheroe
Peter & Jane Cook
Mrs. S. Cooper
Myrtle E. Cox
Barbara F. Cox
Dave Craddock
Peter & Patricia Crick
B. D. & S. M. Crownshaw
Margery Maud Curtin
Betty Dalton
Mrs. Heather R. Davies
James Dyer
Harry & Ann Earl
John & Maisie Edelnand (Edma Jewellers)
Trevor Evans
Lou & Vivienne Evans

Stuart & Jean Farmbrough
Paul Fleet
Eileen & Tony Gatward
Derrick Gilbert
Patricia & John Gillespie
Margaret & Stuart Goodyear
Marion & Tony Hales
Jack & Audrey Harwood
Dennis & Joan Hawkins
Tony & Enid Herbert
Mr. Gerald P. Hodge
Kelvin Hopkins M.P.
Catherine Howe
Peggy & Bob Howe
Mrs. Joyce Hymus
Dorothy Iszatt
Margaret Jackson (née Saunderson)
Beryl M. Jarvis (née Horton)
Mr. Haydon G. Jarvis
Reg & Sylvia Joy (née Gomm)
Alan Keene
Brian Keith Joyner
Roy & Shirley Joyner
Dorothy M. King
Mrs. J. C. King
John M. Lee
T.J. & H. G. Madigan
Pip Manning
Mr. L. J. Martin
Betty Marriott (née Alexander)
Tony & Lynne McKee (née Anderson)
Pam & Des Mead
Mrs. Joan Moulsley
Tom Mower
Pat & Kenn Munslow

Barry P. Neale
Shirley Noller
Claire & Terry Olney
Mrs. P. Patten (née Rogers)
Pauline Pedder (née Alexander)
Sheila Potter (née Gilbert)
Bill Powers
Mrs. Sylvia Rayner
Edna Rippengale
Jill & Alan Robins
Norah & John Robson
Mrs. Monica D. Ronald
Miss Avril M. Sanderson
Mrs. Margaret J. Sanderson
Mr. Paul B. Sanderson
Ken Severn

Mrs. Rosalind A. Shaw
Sally Siddons (née Overhill)
Leslie Sims
Stuart A. Smith
Vicky Stone (née Hall)
Mrs. Y. D. Tomkins
J. C. Walker CMBHI
Richard A. Ward
Rita Whipp (née Gilbert)
Wendy & David White
Stuart Wigg
Tony Wild
Bob Wood
Mrs. Christine Woodhouse (née Arnold)
M. & M. P. Woodridge
Jennifer Wright

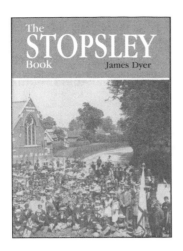
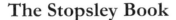

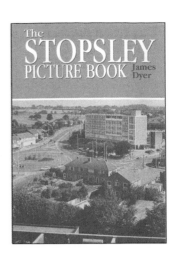

The Stopsley Book

The Stopsley Picture Book

James Dyer

The hamlet of Stopsley, two miles from Luton in Bedfordshire, has a history that stretches back some 300,000 years. Situated in a region initially dependent on agriculture, straw plaiting and brick making, it can be seen as a microcosm 'of life in almost any village on the northern edge of the Chiltern Hills.

The Stopsley Book tells the story of 20 farms, 16 schools and 4 churches within the civil parish which stretched from Someries Castle in the south to Galley Hill and the Icknield Way in the north. It looks in detail at almost every aspect of village life, particularly in the 19th and 20th centuries, and includes the work of the Parish Council, the weather, water and gas supplies, health care, policing, farm work,

brick making and a wide variety of leisure pursuits. Based on thirty years of extensive search and interviews with local people, many now deceased; it is an exhaustive account of a community that still prides itself on its village spirit and individuality.

It includes a collection of 146 photographs, many of which have not been published before.

The Stopsley Book aroused such a great deal of interest in Britain and abroad that a number of readers submitted archive photographs of Stopsley and its surrounding area to the author. These are included in *The Stopsley Picture Book,* which contains 150 photographs and carefully researched captions, to supplement the original work.

The
Book
Castle

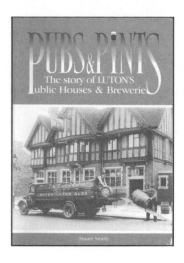

Pubs and Pints

The story of Luton's Public Houses and Breweries

Stuart Smith

Whilst the town of Luton is well documented in other ways, this profusely illustrated book is the first comprehensive history of its important brewing industry and retail beer outlets – linked, staple trades in the area for over five hundred years.

The development of the modern public house from the early taverns and coaching inns closely followed that of the breweries, with the final decades of the last century seen as the high point in the number of houses licensed to sell beers for consumption on or off the premises. Since then the total has declined with the loss of around 40% during the last one hundred years, most of these losses occurring in the period from 1950 to 1970.

Although documentation dealing with the early breweries and public houses is extremely sparse, it is the intention of this book to try and record the history of each brewery and public house that has had its bearing on the social and drinking pastimes of Lutonians over the last one hundred and fifty years. A special feature of this book is the vast range of three hundred photographs – many old, rare and unusual.

A Hatful Of Music

Stuart Goodyear

In 1939 Lutonian Stuart Goodyear was born into a musical household, whose father, also Stuart, encouraged him to embrace his love of music.

As a millennium project, Stuart was asked by the Luton Historical Society to write a page or two about the local "dance band days" of the last century, and drawing on his own involvement as novice pianist through to bandleader, was happy to undertake the challenge.

Starting in a modest way in the 1950s with fellow airport apprentices, his first band The Rainbow Melody Makers, rapidly became a larger and more polished dance band, and was subsequently renamed The Ray Miller Band. Remaining as leader of the band through to the 1980s, he became well connected with the local musical establishment, and has comprehensively collated his experiences during that time, although it soon became apparent that the finished article would be a book, rather than a dossier.

In a most fascinating personal and wider-ranging survey of musical days gone by in Luton, Dunstable and the surrounding area, Stuart has compiled a detailed impression of how he remembered the busy dance scene, and the many brilliant musicians who contributed to a period of live musical entertainment that will never return.

Deliberating over a title, he shortlisted "Batons and Bows" and "You've gotta lot to learn my boy", but thinks that a "Hatful of Music" just about strikes the right chord. The book contains over 300 photos of events covered over the years. People born and bred in Luton will be pouring over the nostalgia for weeks to come.

Barking Mad

Danae Johnston

Every dog lover between nine and ninety will enjoy following the exploits of Tom and Gill, two delinquent poodles.

On their retirement, despite the risk to their prize-winning garden and resident cats, Danae and David rashly take on these canine comedians, their first dogs!

So naïve that they did not know how big the puppies would get, or even that they would need to be clipped at six weekly intervals, the pensioners were to learn everything the hard way – how to deal with scrape after scrape. When Tom jumped the garden fence and returned with one of the neighbours' chickens, for instance! When the dogs herded a flock of sheep into a pond on Christmas Day, or paid an unscheduled visit to a retirement home, or stole the cream from the Jersey milk as it cooled in a bucket on the farmer's kitchen floor, or chased a wallaby at Whipsnade Wild Animal Park- the mischievious adventures go on and on.

Author Danae is a Lutonian, and many of the dogs' exploits are in and around Bedfordshire. Her humorous cartoons and original pithy style make this book a must for all dog lovers. She is also a talented gardener and her garden "Seal Point" has appeared in magazines and on T.V. many times, the most notable being in 1999 when she won the title "B.B.C. Gardener of the Year for the East and South East of England." Many famous gardeners have been to her garden. Geoff Hamilton, back in 1986, Gay Search in 1998, and of course during the recent competition Adam Pasco, Nigel Colborn and Ali Ward as the judges, plus Charlie Dimmock and Alan Titchmarsh, who masterminded the whole show, were around. At certain times her garden is also open to the public to view for charity. And throughout Tom and Gill were never far away!

The Book Castle

The Changing Face of Luton

Stephen Bunker, Robin Holgate & Marian Nichols

"*The Changing Face of Luton*" traces the fortunes of the settlement and economy of the town from the earliest recorded arrival of people in the area to the present day. It looks at different aspects of Luton and its development rather than giving a straight chronological account of its history.

Luton's roots go back a very long way, yet in less than 200 years it has changed from a small market town to today's busy industrial and commercial centre. This transformation is described, helped by a range of excellent photographs, thereby answering many of the questions frequently asked, and perhaps raising more, about this intriguing town.

The three authors from Luton Museum are all experts in local history, archaeology and industry.

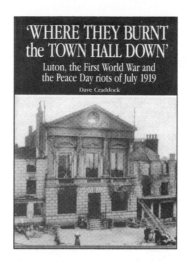

"Where They Burnt the Town Hall Down"

Luton, The First World War and the Peace day Riots of July 1919

Dave Craddock

The weekend of 19/20th July 1919 was arguably the most momentous in the history of Luton. What began as an afternoon of peace celebrations marking the end of the Great War turned into riots that had by the Sunday morning left the Town Hall a smouldering gutted ruin with the military in control of the town. Yet over the years, the story of the riots has been largely neglected.

Drawing broadly on contemporary documents, witness statements and newspaper reports, the book gives a blow-by-blow account of the riots, their aftermath and subsequent trials. The hostility between the Town Council and ex-servicemen's organisations in the preceding months is also covered extensively, as is the impact of the First World War on Luton.

Features of this book include informative appendices containing a wealth of information and over 50 illustrations.

Exploring History All Around

Vivienne Evans

A handbook of local history, arranged as a series of routes to cover Bedfordshire and adjoining parts of Hertfordshire and Buckinghamshire. It is organised as two books in one. There are seven thematic sections full of fascinating historical detail and anecdotes for armchair reading. Also it is a perfect source of family days out as the book is organised as circular motoring/ cycling explorations, highlighting attractions and landmarks. Also included is a background history to all the major towns in the area, plus dozens of villages, which will enhance your appreciation and understanding of the history that is all around you!